YOUR PERSONAL

ASTROLOGY

GUIDE

VIRGO
2013

YOUR PERSONAL
ASTROLOGY
GUIDE

VIRGO
2013

RICK LEVINE **& JEFF** JAWER

STERLING ETHOS
New York

STERLING ETHOS
New York

An Imprint of Sterling Publishing
387 Park Avenue South
New York, NY 10016

© 2012 by Sterling Publishing Co., Inc.
Text © 2012 by Rick Levine and Jeff Jawer

ISBN 978-1-4027-7965-7

Distributed in Canada by Sterling Publishing
c/o Canadian Manda Group, 165 Dufferin Street
Toronto, Ontario, Canada M6K 3H6
Distributed in the United Kingdom by GMC Distribution Services
Castle Place, 166 High Street, Lewes, East Sussex, England BN7 1XU
Distributed in Australia by Capricorn Link (Australia) Pty. Ltd.
P.O. Box 704, Windsor, NSW 2756, Australia

For information about custom editions, special sales, and premium
and corporate purchases, please contact Sterling Special Sales at
800-805-5489 or specialsales@sterlingpublishing.com.

Manufactured in the United States of America

2 4 6 8 10 9 7 5 3 1

www.sterlingpublishing.com

TABLE OF CONTENTS

Author's Note:

Your Personal Astrology Guide uses the Tropical zodiac based on the seasons, not the constellations. This method of determining signs has been and continues to be the practice of Western astrologers for over 2,000 years. Aries, the beginning of the Tropical zodiac, starts on the first day of spring every year. Contrary to what you may have heard, no one's sign has changed, regardless of when you were born and the addition of a thirteenth sign is not relevant to Western astrology.

Measuring and recording the apparent movement of the Sun, the Moon, and the planets against the backdrop of the heavens is a complex task because nothing is stationary. Even the location of the constellations with respect to the seasons gradually changes from year to year. Since astrologers are concerned with human behavior here on Earth, they created a twelve-fold zodiac that is anchored to four seasons as their primary frame of reference. Obviously, astrologers fully understand that there are eighty-eight official constellations and that the moving planets travel through many of them (including Ophiuchus and Orion), but these are not—and never have been—part of the Tropical zodiac created by astrologers.

THE PURPOSE OF THIS BOOK

The more you learn about yourself, the better able you are to wisely use the energies in your life.
For more than 3,000 years, astrology has been the sharpest tool in the box for describing the human condition. Used by virtually every culture on the planet, astrology continues to serve as a link between individual lives and planetary cycles. We gain valuable insights into personal issues with a birth chart, and can plot the patterns of the year ahead in meaningful ways for individuals as well as groups. You share your sun sign with eight percent of humanity. Clearly, you're not all going to have the same day, even if the basic astrological cycles are the same. Your individual circumstances, the specific factors of your entire birth chart, and your own free will help you write your unique story.

The purpose of this book is to describe the energies of the Sun, Moon, and planets for the year ahead and help you create your future, rather than being a victim of it. We facilitate your journey by showing you the turns ahead in the road of life and hopefully the best ways to navigate them.

YOU ARE THE STAR
OF YOUR LIFE

It is not our goal to simply predict events. Rather, we are reporting the planetary energies—the cosmic weather in which you are living—so that you understand these conditions and know how to use them most effectively.

The power, though, isn't in the stars, but in your mind, your heart, and the choices that you make every day. Regardless of how strongly you are buffeted by the winds of change or bored by stagnation, you have many ways to view any situation. Learning about the energies of the Sun, Moon, and planets will both sharpen and widen your perspective, thereby giving you additional choices.

The language of astrology is a gift of awareness, not a rigid set of rules. It works best when blended with common sense, intuition, and self-trust. This is your life, and no one knows how to live it as well as you. Take what you need from this book and leave the rest. Although the planets set the stage for the year ahead, you're the writer, director, and star of your life and you can play the part in whatever way you choose. *Your Personal Astrology Guide* uses information about your sun sign to give you a better understanding of how the planetary waves will wash upon your shore. We each navigate our lives through time, and each moment has unique qualities. Astrology gives us the ability to describe the constantly changing timescape. For example, if you know the trajectory and the speed of an approaching storm, you can choose to delay a leisurely afternoon sail on the bay, thus avoiding an unpleasant situation.

By reading this book, you can improve your ability to align with the cosmic weather, the larger patterns that affect you day to day. You can become more effective by aligning with the cosmos and cocreating the year ahead with a better understanding of the energies around you.

Astrology doesn't provide quick fixes to life's complex issues. It doesn't offer neatly packed black-and-white answers in a world filled with an infinite variety of shapes and colors. It can, however, give you a much clearer picture of the invisible forces influencing your life.

ENERGY & EVENTS

Two sailboats can face the same gale yet travel in opposite directions as a result of how the sails are positioned. Similarly, how you respond to the energy of a particular set of circumstances may be more responsible for your fate than the given situation itself. We delineate the energetic winds for your year ahead, but your attitude shapes the unfolding events, and your responses alter your destiny.

This book emphasizes the positive, not because all is good, but because astrology shows us ways to transform even the power of a storm into beneficial results. Empowerment comes from learning to see the invisible energy patterns that impact the visible landscape as you fill in the details of your story every day on this spinning planet, orbited by the Moon, lit by the Sun, and colored by the nuances of the planets.

You are a unique point in an infinite galaxy of unlimited possibilities, and the choices that you make have consequences. So use this book in a most magical way to consciously improve your life.

MOON CHARTS

2013 NEW MOONS

Each New Moon marks the beginning of a cycle. In general, this is the best time to plant seeds for future growth. Use the days preceeding the New Moon to finish old business prior to starting what comes next. The focused mind can be quite sharp during this phase. Harness the potential of the New Moon by stating your intentions—out loud or in writing—for the weeks ahead. Hold these goals in your mind and help them grow to fruition through conscious actions as the Moon gains light during the following two weeks. In the chart below, the dates and times refer to when the Moon and Sun align in each zodiac sign (see p. 16), initiating a new lunar cycle.

DATE	TIME	SIGN
January 11	2:43 pm EST	Capricorn
February 10	2:20 am EST	Aquarius
March 11	3:51 pm EDT	Pisces
April 10	5:35 am EDT	Aries
May 9	8:28 pm EDT	Taurus (ECLIPSE)
June 8	11:56 am EDT	Gemini
July 8	3:14 am EDT	Cancer
August 6	5:50 pm EDT	Leo
September 5	7:36 am EDT	Virgo
October 4	8:34 pm EDT	Libra
November 3	7:49 am EST	Scorpio (ECLIPSE)
December 2	7:22 pm EST	Sagittarius

2013 FULL MOONS

The Full Moon reflects the light of the Sun as subjective feelings reflect the objective events of the day. Dreams seem bigger; moods feel stronger. Emotional waters run with deeper currents. This is the phase of culmination, a turning point in the energetic cycle. Now it's time to listen to the inner voices. Rather than starting new projects, the two weeks after the Full Moon are when we complete what we can and slow our outward expressions in anticipation of the next New Moon. In this chart, the dates and times refer to when the moon is opposite the sun in each zodiac sign, marking the emotional peak of each lunar cycle.

DATE	TIME	SIGN
January 26	11:38 pm EST	Leo
February 25	3:26 pm EST	Virgo
March 27	5:27 am EDT	Libra
April 25	3:57 pm EDT	Scorpio (ECLIPSE)
May 25	12:24 am EDT	Sagittarius
June 23	7:32 am EDT	Capricorn
July 22	2:15 pm EDT	Aquarius
August 20	9:44 pm EDT	Aquarius
September 19	7:12 am EDT	Pisces
October 18	7:37 pm EDT	Aries (ECLIPSE)
November 17	10:15 am EST	Taurus
December 17	4:28 am EST	Gemini

ASTROLOGY,
YOU & THE
WORLD

WELCOME TO YOUR SUN SIGN

The Sun, Moon, and Earth and all the planets lie within a plane called the **ecliptic** and move through a narrow band of stars made up by 12 constellations called the **zodiac**. The Earth revolves around the Sun once a year, but from our point of view, it appears that the Sun moves through each sign of the zodiac for one month. There are 12 months and astrologically there are 12 signs. The astrological months, however, do not match our calendar, and start between the 19th and 23rd of each month. Everyone is born to an astrological month, like being born in a room with a particular perspective of the world. Knowing your sun sign provides useful information about your personality and your future, but for a more detailed astrological analysis, a full birth chart calculation based on your precise date, time, and place of birth is necessary. Get your complete birth chart online at:

http://www.tarot.com/astrology/astroprofile

This book is about your zodiac sign. Your Sun
in the earth sign of efficient Virgo is analytical
and practical. You excel at separating the wheat
from the chaff, the valuable kernel from the rest.
As such, you can be highly discriminating, even
critical. You're a careful perfectionist in your work.
Your greatest strength is being able to apply what
you know to serve others. More than anything, you
want to be useful.

THE PLANETS

We refer to the Sun and Moon as planets. Don't
worry; we do know about modern astronomy.
Although the Sun is really a star and the Moon is
a satellite, they are called planets for astrological
purposes. The astrological planets are the Sun,
the Moon, Mercury, Venus, Mars, Jupiter, Saturn,
Chiron, Uranus, Neptune, and Pluto.

Your sun sign is the most obvious astrological
placement, for the Sun returns to the same sign
every year. But at the same time, the Moon is
orbiting the Earth, changing signs every two and
a third days. Mercury, Venus, and Mars each move
through a sign in a few weeks to a few months.

Jupiter spends a whole year in a sign—and Pluto visits a sign for up to 30 years! The ever-changing positions of the planets alter the energetic terrain through which we travel. The planets are symbols; each has a particular range of meanings. For example, Venus is the goddess of love, but it really symbolizes beauty in a spectrum of experiences. Venus can represent romantic love, sensuality, the arts, or good food. It activates anything that we value, including personal possessions and even money. To our ancestors, the planets actually animated life on Earth. In this way of thinking, every beautiful flower contains the essence of Venus.

Each sign has a natural affinity to an individual planet, and as this planet moves through the sky, it sends messages of particular interest to people born under that sign. Your key or ruling planet is Mercury, the Messenger of the Heavens. Quicksilver Mercury is the fastest of the true planets, symbolic of the speed and changeability of thought. Its movement shows the qualities of your thinking process and speech. Planets can be described by many different words, for the mythology of each is a rich tapestry. In this book we use a variety of words when talking about each planet in order to convey the most applicable meaning. The table below describes a few keywords for each planet, including the Sun and Moon.

PLANET	SYMBOL	KEYWORDS
Sun	☉	Consciousness, Will, Vitality
Moon	☽	Subconscious, Emotions, Habits
Mercury	☿	Communication, Thoughts, Transportation
Venus	♀	Desire, Love, Money, Values
Mars	♂	Action, Physical Energy, Drive
Jupiter	♃	Expansion, Growth, Optimism
Saturn	♄	Contraction, Maturity, Responsibility
Chiron	⚷	Healing, Pain, Subversion
Uranus	♅	Awakening, Unpredictable, Inventive
Neptune	♆	Imagination, Spirituality, Confusion
Pluto	♇	Passion, Intensity, Regeneration

HOUSES

Just as planets move through the signs of the zodiac, they also move through the houses in an individual chart. The 12 houses correspond to the 12 signs, but are individualized, based upon your sign. In this book we use Solar Houses, which place your sun sign in your 1st House. Therefore, when a planet enters a new sign it also enters a new house. If you know your exact time of birth, the rising sign determines the 1st House. You can learn your rising sign by entering your birth date at:

http://www.tarot.com/astrology/astroprofile

HOUSE	SIGN	KEYWORDS
1st House	Aries	Self, Appearance, Personality
2nd House	Taurus	Possessions, Values, Self-Worth
3rd House	Gemini	Communication, Siblings, Short Trips
4th House	Cancer	Home, Family, Roots
5th House	Leo	Love, Romance, Children, Play
6th House	Virgo	Work, Health, Daily Routines
7th House	Libra	Marriage, Relationships, Business Partners
8th House	Scorpio	Intimacy, Transformation, Shared Resources
9th House	Sagittarius	Travel, Higher Education, Philosophy
10th House	Capricorn	Career, Community, Ambition
11th House	Aquarius	Groups and Friends, Associations, Social Ideals
12th House	Pisces	Imagination, Spirituality, Secret Activities

ASPECTS

As the planets move through the sky in their various cycles, they form ever-changing angles with one another. Certain angles create significant geometric shapes. So, when two planets are 90 degrees apart, they conform to a square; 60 degrees of separation conforms to a sextile, or six-pointed star. Planets create **aspects** when they're at these special angles. Aspects explain how the individual symbolism of pairs of planets combine into an energetic pattern.

ASPECT	DEGREES	KEYWORD
Conjunction	0	Compression, Blending, Focus
Opposition	180	Tension, Awareness, Balance
Trine	120	Harmony, Free-Flowing, Ease
Square	90	Resistance, Stress, Dynamic Conflict
Quintile	72	Creativity, Metaphysical, Magic
Sextile	60	Support, Intelligent, Activating
Quincunx	150	Irritation, Annoyance, Adjustment

2013 GENERAL FORECAST

Astrology works for individuals, groups, and humanity as a whole. You will have your own story in 2013, but it will unfold along with seven billion other tales of human experience. We are each unique, yet our lives touch one another; our destinies are woven together by weather and war, by the economy, science, music, politics, religion, and all the other threads of life on planet Earth.

This astrological look at the major trends and planetary patterns for 2013 provides a framework for comprehending the potentials and challenges we face together, so that we can move forward with tolerance and respect as a community as we also fulfill our potential as individuals.

The astrological events used for this forecast are the transits of major planets Jupiter and Saturn, the retrograde cycles of Mercury, and the eclipses of the Sun and the Moon.

A NOTE ABOUT DATES IN THIS BOOK

All events are based upon the Eastern Time Zone of the United States. Because of local time differences, an event occurring just a few minutes after midnight in the East will actually happen the prior day in the rest of the country. Although the key dates are the exact dates of any particular alignment, some of you are so ready for certain things to happen that you can react to a transit a day or two before it is exact. And sometimes you can be so entrenched in habits or unwilling to change that you may not notice the effects right away. Allow extra time around each key date to feel the impact of any event.

JUPITER IN GEMINI:
LARGER THAN LIFE
June 11, 2012–June 25, 2013

Astrological tradition considers multifaceted Gemini an awkward place for truth-seeking Jupiter. We can be inundated with so much information that it's nearly impossible to see the forest for the trees. Jupiter's long-range vision may be obscured by a million and one ideas that scatter attention, diffusing the focus we need to achieve long-term goals. Yes, this mind-opening transit stirs curiosity about a wide variety of subjects—but it may be difficult to concentrate and gain in-depth knowledge in any one area if we're skimming the surface. Expansive Jupiter in communicative Gemini can also be quite verbose, valuing the volume of information more than its substance. Philosophical flexibility and mental versatility are gifts of this transit, while its less desirable qualities include inconsistency of beliefs and careless planning.

JUPITER IN CANCER:
FEELING IS BELIEVING
June 25, 2013–July 16, 2014

Philosophical Jupiter provides understanding through emotions during its stay in sensitive Cancer. We're likely to reject ideas that do not correspond to gut instincts, applying a subjective check against concepts that sound good but just don't feel right. Returning to traditional sources of wisdom and reconnecting with nature and family deepens our roots in the past to provide a needed sense of stability in these tumultuous times. Yet looking back for answers to today's questions has its limitations; conditions are changing so rapidly now that old rules no longer apply. We gain a sense of safety by relying on time-tested principles, but we may lose the potential for envisioning a creative new tomorrow by following these well-worn paths. The sentimental nature of Jupiter in Cancer favors familiar circles to unfamiliar. Given this transit's protective qualities, this makes it easier to justify closing the door to new people and experiences. Racism, nationalism, and religious and ethnic prejudices are more prevalent when mental gates close to outsiders. Yet Jupiter in nurturing Cancer, at its highest potential, helps us recognize the living nature of truth in an ever-growing spiral that draws upon the best of the old to nourish new goals and aspirations.

SATURN IN SCORPIO:
SHADOWBOXING
October 5, 2012–December 23, 2014
June 14, 2015–September 16, 2015

Responsible Saturn in formidable Scorpio tests our resolve. We are challenged to look into the dark corners of our psyches where fears about love, money, and mortality hide. It's tempting to turn away from these complicated subjects, yet the price of doing so is high because we are then controlled by unconscious impulses. Saturn in Scorpio reminds us that no one is entirely pure and simple. The complexities of giving and receiving affection, dealing with hidden desires, and working with manipulative people are numerous. But if we're willing to show up and do the work, Saturn also offers clarity and authority, enabling us to address these complicated matters. Taking responsibility for dark feelings doesn't mean that we must suppress them; it's a signal to engage them with patience rather than punishment. Personal and professional alliances work more effectively when we stop keeping secrets from ourselves. Finally, with Saturn in Scorpio we could see even more consolidation of financial institutions as a result of bad loans.

MERCURY RETROGRADES
February 23–March 17 in Pisces / June 26–July 20 in Cancer / October 21–November 10 in Scorpio

All true planets appear to move backward from time to time, because we view them from the moving platform of Earth. The most noticeable and regular retrograde periods are those of

Mercury, the communication planet. Occurring three or four times a year for roughly three weeks at a time, these are periods when difficulties with details, travel, communication, and technical matters are more common than usual.

Mercury's retrograde is often perceived as negative, but you can make this cycle work for you. Because personal and commercial interactions are emphasized, you can actually accomplish more than usual, especially if you stay focused on what you need to complete instead of initiating new projects. Still, you may feel as if you're treading water—or worse, being carried backward in an undertow of unfinished business. Worry less about making progress than about the quality of your work. Pay extra attention to all your communication exchanges. Avoiding misunderstandings and omissions is the ideal way to minimize complications. Retrograde Mercury is best used to tie up loose ends as you review, redo, reconsider, and, in general, revisit the past.

All three Mercury retrograde cycles occur in emotional water signs this year. This can make communication more difficult, because it's not easy to translate feelings into words. Our potential loss of objectivity, as well, can lead to even more misunderstandings than usual. Thankfully, these three periods give us the chance to reconnect with our emotions, which can inspire new waves of creativity.

ECLIPSES
Solar: May 9 and November 3
Lunar: April 25, May 25, and October 18

Solar and Lunar Eclipses are special New and Full Moons that indicate significant changes for individuals and groups. They are powerful markers of events, with influences that can appear up to three months in advance and last up to six months afterward.

April 25, Lunar Eclipse in Scorpio: Sink or Swim
This Lunar Eclipse in passionate Scorpio tells us to let go of the past and start living in the present. Taskmaster Saturn's conjunction to the Moon, though, encourages a tenacious attitude that can keep us entangled in unrewarding relationships. Resentment, jealousy, and revenge aren't worth the effort they take to sustain. However, initiating

Mars is conjunct to the sensible Taurus Sun, which favors simplifying life and making a fresh start instead of trying to fix an unresolvable problem.

May 9, Solar Eclipse in Taurus: Trim the Fat
The cost of comfort may become so high that we have to let go of laziness or of some luxuries to make life more affordable. There's a self-indulgent side to Taurus, and with combative Mars and talkative Mercury joined with the Sun and Moon, we can find ourselves aggressively defending our behavior. Yet trying to justify standing still and holding on to what we have may only increase the steep price we pay later for resisting the purging we need now.

May 25, Lunar Eclipse in Sagittarius:
Life's an Adventure
An eclipse in farsighted Sagittarius reminds us to bring our attention back from some distant vision to focus on the here and now. We can discover alternative ways to make life work instead of acting as if there's only one road to fulfillment. Beliefs may not hold up in the face of changing

circumstances that require flexibility instead of certainty. Asking questions reveals options that multiply choices, creating confusion for some but freeing most of us from rigid thinking and excessive judgment.

October 18, Lunar Eclipse in Aries:
No Man Is an Island
Life is not a solo voyage even when we're feeling all alone. This eclipse emphasizes the need to work with others and demands some degree of compromise and accommodation. It's better to sit on the fence, gather more information, and mull things over than to race ahead impulsively now. While it may seem that sharing feelings with others hinders progress, it garners us support that overcomes the isolation of not accepting advice and assistance.

November 3, Solar Eclipse in Scorpio: Baby Steps
Expect power struggles controlling Saturn's conjunction to this New Moon Eclipse. It's not easy to trust people—and sometimes it's just as difficult to trust ourselves. This eclipse, however, is about backing away from pressure, reducing

intensity, and seeking peaceful moments in our lives. Recognizing the gifts that we're given every day can alleviate a profound feeling of hunger, perhaps even despair, through small moments of joy and pleasure.

THE BOTTOM LINE:
YELL FIRE!

The Mayan calendar may have turned over near the end of 2012, but the human story on this planet is far from complete. Nevertheless, we are still in the midst of a period of powerful change that began with the opposition of structural Saturn and explosive Uranus in late 2008, when we experienced the first wave of the worst financial crisis since the Great Depression, along with the subsequent election of Barack Obama. The year 2012 brought the first of seven tense squares between Uranus and transformational Pluto that will recur through 2015, shaking the very foundations of societies around the world. The volatile Uranus-Pluto square is exact on May 20 and November 1, April 21 and December 15, 2014, and March 16, 2015. The long-lasting connection between revolutionary Uranus and volcanic Pluto is already fomenting change on a grand scale, and this will continue for years to come.

It is tempting, though, to gaze back and seek to re-create the relative safety of the past. Joyful Jupiter's entry into cautious and conservative Cancer will bring waves of nostalgia for the "good old days," along with protectionist calls for stronger national borders. Yet the idea that we can return to the past is not a feasible one. The technological cats are out of the bag, and addressing environmental issues alone requires forward, not backward, thinking. Our challenge is to construct new realities based on bold visions and idealistic dreams of a world that does not yet exist. This takes courage in the face of confusion and confidence in the midst of chaos. It's tempting to call out to higher powers to rescue us from the consequences of our actions: suffering evokes cries for help. And yet we are capable of healing ourselves if we finally embrace the twenty-first century instead of retreating to mythical moments of an idealized past.

Inventive Uranus in pioneering Aries is opening new neural pathways that are reshaping our view of reality. Yes, we may encounter moments

when thoughts are so strange that we may
fear ourselves to be mad. But curious minds,
flexible egos, and adaptable emotions allow us
to glimpse a more enlightened, evolved, and
competent humanity without breaking down. We
are challenged to dance with the stranger who
enters our heads with perceptions that don't
readily fit into our existing intellectual framework.
We must find new ways out of the dilemmas that
we've created for ourselves. Embracing small
discoveries and appreciating surprises are good
training techniques: they prepare us to step up
to the next level of human evolution and continue
the remarkable journey of love and light on planet
Earth.

Remember that all of these astrological events
are part of the general cosmic weather of the year,
but will affect us each differently based upon our
individual astrological signs.

VIRGO
AUGUST–DECEMBER
2012 OVERVIEW

STARTING OVER

Your life gets back on track this month as you are finally ready to move from fixing the past to creating the future. This change begins when your ruling planet, Mercury, turns direct on **August 8**, freeing up mindshare to consider new ideas and projects. On **August 22**, the Sun enters Virgo, warming your sign with confidence and courage for the next thirty days. Managing your job and physical well-being could be key areas for breakthroughs with the progressive Aquarius Full Moon on **August 1** brightening your 6th House of Health and Work. However, the push toward innovation is partially countered by lovable Venus's entry into cautious Cancer and your 11th House of Groups on **August 7**. This can bring you comfort from friends and colleagues, but your need for security and a strong sense of loyalty may stop you from taking chances or making dramatic changes.

A rising force of enthusiasm rushes in with the New Moon in proud Leo on **August 17**. This lunation occurs in your 12th House of Spiritual Mystery, so you might feel the growing wave of energy before you understand where it's heading. This powerful Sun-Moon conjunction is supported by sextiles to productive Mars and Saturn, ensuring that you can translate whatever inspiration you find into decisive action. On **August 23**, you get another shot of energy when dynamic Mars dives into emotionally driven Scorpio and your 3rd House of Information, reinforcing the impetus you get from the Sun in Virgo and helping you eliminate obstacles and frivolous tasks so you can focus on your most important goals. A magical Pisces Full Moon joins ethereal Neptune in your 7th House of Partners on the **31st**, inspiring relationship dreams or illusions.

WEDNESDAY 1 ★ ○ Develop new skills and interests

THURSDAY 2	
FRIDAY 3	
SATURDAY 4	
SUNDAY 5	
MONDAY 6	
TUESDAY 7	

WEDNESDAY 8 ★ Feelings are more important than facts

THURSDAY 9 ★	
FRIDAY 10	
SATURDAY 11	
SUNDAY 12	
MONDAY 13	
TUESDAY 14	

WEDNESDAY 15 ★ Dig below the surface to uncover hidden resources

---

THURSDAY 16	
FRIDAY 17	●
SATURDAY 18	
SUNDAY 19	
MONDAY 20	
TUESDAY 21	

WEDNESDAY 22 ★ **SUPER NOVA DAYS** Overlook petty differences

---

THURSDAY 23 ★	
FRIDAY 24 ★	
SATURDAY 25	
SUNDAY 26	
MONDAY 27	
TUESDAY 28	

WEDNESDAY 29 ★ Put a positive spin on a negative situation

THURSDAY 30	
FRIDAY 31	○

★ designates key date

ORGANIZED CHAOS

You have a strong sense of purpose and a cohesive plan to reach your goals as the month begins. The willful Sun in your sign until **September 22** empowers you to act more boldly and creatively, while meticulous Mercury in Virgo focuses your mind to fill in the details and refine systems that support your ambitions. This intense concentration can narrow your thinking and blur your perception of the big picture. When surprises happen—and they will—it's important to look up from your little piece of the puzzle to adapt to the bigger changes in the world around you. The Virgo New Moon on **September 15** is joined with Mercury in your 1st House of Physicality, reminding you to maintain a healthy diet and exercise program. But this lunation also can spur you to take the initiative in relationships and to launch new projects. However, it's essential to be open to alternative points of view once Mercury moves into diplomatic Libra and your 6th House of Work on the **16th**. Making compromises to meet others halfway during this period is more useful than rigidly adhering to your own ideas.

The second of seven life-altering Uranus-Pluto squares occurs on **September 19**. The shocks represented by this long-term pattern, occurring intermittently until **March 16, 2015**, are triggered on **September 20–29** by fast-moving planets that make you acutely aware of what's holding you back. Difficult aspects from Mercury, Mars, Venus, and the Sun can spark sudden shifts in your mood and surprising changes in the current circumstances. Relationships are on shaky ground on the **29th** when the reckless Aries Full Moon squares ruthless Pluto and joins unpredictable Uranus in your 8th House of Intimacy.

SEPTEMBER 2012

SATURDAY 1 ★ Explore your imagination

SUNDAY 2

MONDAY 3

TUESDAY 4

WEDNESDAY 5

THURSDAY 6

FRIDAY 7 ★ You might raise expectations beyond reason

SATURDAY 8 ★

SUNDAY 9 ★

MONDAY 10 ★

TUESDAY 11

WEDNESDAY 12

THURSDAY 13

FRIDAY 14

SATURDAY 15 ●

SUNDAY 16

MONDAY 17

TUESDAY 18

WEDNESDAY 19

THURSDAY 20 ★ **SUPER NOVA DAYS** Conversations grow convoluted

---

FRIDAY 21 ★

SATURDAY 22 ★

SUNDAY 23

MONDAY 24

TUESDAY 25 ★ Your extreme desires could prompt risky behavior

---

WEDNESDAY 26 ★

THURSDAY 27

FRIDAY 28

SATURDAY 29 ★ ○ Create an escape plan that's both safe and stimulating

---

SUNDAY 30

BEAUTY AND THE BOTTOM LINE

Your willingness to make tough decisions now will make your life easier in the future. If you've been wavering about financial matters, this is the right time to tune in to your gut feelings, get off the fence, and take decisive action. The Sun illuminates your 2nd House of Resources until **October 22**, providing you with ample opportunities to weigh your budgetary options. It helps if your choices are rooted in self-confidence, which thankfully receives a boost when attractive Venus enters Virgo on **October 3**. Your charming personality, creative approach, and sense of style should turn heads in your direction with this alluring transit. Yet the refined qualities of Venus in Virgo are contrasted with an adventurous spirit when courageous Mars enters Sagittarius and your 4th House of Roots on **October 6**. While you keep up appearances of commitment to your current situation, Mars at the bottom of your chart can incite conflict at home if you're feeling hemmed in or bored.

On **October 10**, the first beneficial trine of pragmatic Saturn and whimsical Neptune occurs. You can combine your thoughtful analyses with romantic impulses, solidifying an inspiring partnership. These aspects return on **June 11** and **July 19, 2013**, to manifest the dreams that are now taking shape. The Sun's dive into psychologically astute Scorpio on **October 22** takes your thinking to another level, inviting profound conversations and serious research. The pressure of the Sun's conjunction to restrictive Saturn on the **25th** can temporarily block the flow of communication and sow seeds of doubt. Happily, lovely Venus restores your sense of self-worth on **October 28** with her entry into sociable Libra and your resourceful 2nd House.

MONDAY 1

TUESDAY 2

WEDNESDAY 3

THURSDAY 4

FRIDAY 5 ★ Words take on extra significance

SATURDAY 6 ★

SUNDAY 7 ★

MONDAY 8

TUESDAY 9

WEDNESDAY 10

THURSDAY 11

FRIDAY 12

SATURDAY 13

SUNDAY 14

MONDAY 15 ★ ● Restrain the urge to splurge

TUESDAY 16

WEDNESDAY 17

THURSDAY 18

FRIDAY 19

SATURDAY 20 ★ Don't stress if you can't put your thoughts into words

SUNDAY 21 ★

MONDAY 22

TUESDAY 23

WEDNESDAY 24

THURSDAY 25 ★ SUPER NOVA DAY Withholding information undermines trust

FRIDAY 26

SATURDAY 27

SUNDAY 28 ★ Keep your head in the clouds and your feet on the ground

MONDAY 29 ★ ○

TUESDAY 30

WEDNESDAY 31

USEFUL U-TURN

You're better off taking a few steps back this month than forging straight ahead. Your ruling planet, Mercury, turns retrograde on **November 6** and continues in reverse until the **26th**. This cycle starts in outgoing Sagittarius and your domestic 4th House and ends in introspective Scorpio in your 3rd House of Information. Review and revise big plans and expectations, especially related to home and family; you may have overlooked data that's critical to your success. It can be frustrating to reassess and, perhaps, rebuild, but this extra effort will ultimately streamline your thinking and reduce complications. Two eclipses in November also remind you to let go if you want to grow.

The New Moon in Scorpio on **November 13** is a Solar Eclipse in your 3rd House of Immediate Environment. Normally, the monthly conjunction of the Sun and Moon is a launching pad—in this case for learning, research, and communication. However, this eclipse also tells you to simplify data, eliminate superfluous ideas, and concentrate on key people and points instead of overloading yourself with input. The momentum starts to shift with the Sun's entry into adventurous Sagittarius on the **21st** and Mercury's forward turn on the **26th**. Then, on **November 28**, the jittery Gemini Full Moon is a Lunar Eclipse activating your 10th House of Career. Prosperous Jupiter's conjunction to the Moon and a square from fantasy-prone Neptune inspire professional dreams with promises that stretch the bounds of credibility. Avoid chasing an illusion by questioning your assumptions and those of people offering something that sounds too good to be true.

THURSDAY 1 ★ Finances take a sudden turn

FRIDAY 2 ★

SATURDAY 3 ★

SUNDAY 4

MONDAY 5

TUESDAY 6

WEDNESDAY 7

THURSDAY 8

FRIDAY 9

SATURDAY 10

SUNDAY 11 ★ Avoid paranoia by keeping your beliefs grounded in reality

---

MONDAY 12 ★

TUESDAY 13 ★ ●

WEDNESDAY 14

THURSDAY 15

FRIDAY 16 ★ Concentrate on activities that have the most impact

---

SATURDAY 17 ★

SUNDAY 18

MONDAY 19

TUESDAY 20

WEDNESDAY 21

THURSDAY 22 ★ Follow standard operating procedures

FRIDAY 23 ★

SATURDAY 24 ★

SUNDAY 25

MONDAY 26 ★ **SUPER NOVA DAYS** Harsh judgment demands strong action

---

TUESDAY 27 ★

WEDNESDAY 28 ★ ○

THURSDAY 29

FRIDAY 30

SPREAD YOUR WINGS AND FLY

Family matters take on deep significance this holiday season, especially with several planets moving through your 4th House of Roots. Loquacious Mercury arrives on **December 10**, spurring frank speech and strong opinions. The ebullient Sagittarius New Moon on **December 13** is also in your 4th House and can inspire a fresh start, compelling you to enlarge your space or consider a move to a larger place. Its higher purpose, though, is to motivate you to look beyond the limits of your current surroundings to imagine a more enlivening personal or professional life. The forward turn of revolutionary Uranus in your 6th House of Work on the same day underscores your need to get more stimulation from your job. Vivacious Venus dances into Sagittarius and your 4th House on the **15th**. This joyous planet sweetens your experiences by helping you look beyond the limitations of the present to visualize a more rewarding future.

Generous Jupiter's quincunxes to shrewd Pluto on the **20th** and stingy Saturn on the **22nd** remind you that every gain comes at a price. Although the final bills will not be due until these aspects finish on **March 23–29, 2013**, potential new resources will soon be available to you. On **December 21**, the Winter Solstice is marked by the Sun's entry into industrious Capricorn and your 5th House of Creativity, where you can reorganize and apply your talents more effectively. Active Mars's move into inventive Aquarius and your 6th House of Skills on the **25th** pushes you to update your techniques or develop new ones. On **December 26**, a savvy Saturn-Pluto sextile, returning on **March 8** and **September 21, 2013**, helps you to apply your force with precision and purpose.

SATURDAY 1 ★ You're likely to go too far or expect too much

SUNDAY 2 ★

MONDAY 3

TUESDAY 4

WEDNESDAY 5

THURSDAY 6

FRIDAY 7

SATURDAY 8

SUNDAY 9

MONDAY 10 ★ Your imagination soars as communications grow confusing

---

TUESDAY 11 ★

WEDNESDAY 12 ★

THURSDAY 13 ●

FRIDAY 14

SATURDAY 15

SUNDAY 16 ★ Strong messages conflict with hypersensitivity

MONDAY 17 ★

TUESDAY 18

WEDNESDAY 19

THURSDAY 20

FRIDAY 21 ★ Take the lead in romantic matters

SATURDAY 22 ★

SUNDAY 23

MONDAY 24

TUESDAY 25

WEDNESDAY 26

THURSDAY 27

FRIDAY 28 ★ ○ **SUPER NOVA DAYS** Your self-expression may be extreme

---

SATURDAY 29 ★

SUNDAY 30 ★

MONDAY 31

2013 HOROSCOPE

VIRGO

AUGUST 23–SEPTEMBER 22

OVERVIEW OF THE YEAR

Putting your life in perfect order is overwhelming if you try to do it all at once. So start small and work your way up to the bigger issues this year; you'll make great strides in your ongoing journey of self-improvement. Responsible Saturn is in your 3rd House of Immediate Environment, requiring you to restructure your day-to-day life and how you interact with those closest to you. **Instead of letting your philosophical perspective dictate your daily agenda, be as mindful as possible with every little thing you do.** Pay more attention to how you manage the flow of information in your communication with others. You can refine the way you talk and how you listen by being more conscious of your own mental patterns and habitual behaviors. You become even more serious about this process when transformational Pluto forms a supportive sextile to Saturn on March 8 and September 21 in a series that began on December 26, 2012.

Other people are a source of inspiration this year, although you need to establish solid

boundaries if you're to remain clear about your goals. With imaginative Neptune camped out in your 7th House of Relationships, those closest to you can act as mirrors reflecting your own fantasies. However, confusion dissipates on June 11 and July 19 when hardworking Saturn harmoniously trines Neptune, enabling you to take very practical steps toward realizing your dreams. Additional emotional support comes from five other planets moving through your 11th House of Friends during June and July, creating a series of auspicious grand trines. On June 3–7, communicator Mercury and sweet Venus complete a Grand Water Trine with Saturn and Neptune, turning on your charisma, increasing your powers of persuasion, and prompting others to support your aspirations. At the end of the month, it's the Sun's turn to radiate emotional security as it trines Saturn and Neptune on June 26. Your confidence and enthusiasm are off the charts when buoyant Jupiter and impulsive Mars reactivate this magical planetary pattern on July 17–20. During this phase, your overall sense of well-being can be very satisfying—but don't grow complacent,

because this is a propitious time to put your
plans into motion.

Personal relationships remain in the spotlight
as the long-lasting square between wayward
Uranus in your 8th House of Regeneration and
passionate Pluto in your 5th House of Love and
Creativity is exact on May 20 and November 1.
This aspect series, which began on June 24, 2012,
and completes on March 16, 2015, can revitalize
a flagging partnership if you're willing to engage
in deep psychological transformation. However,
it can also signal the end of a relationship if you
are fearfully clinging to the past and unwilling
to make any changes. In either case, your desire
for independence will be strong enough to
make waves when honorable Saturn forms an
irritable quincunx with irrepressible Uranus on
April 12 and October 5 in a series that began on
November 15, 2012.

HOUSE OF MIRRORS

Your analytical ability may not help you as you attempt to understand your relationships this year. Mystical Neptune's presence in your 7th House of Others can put an enchanting spell on any partnership. However, it can also create a layer of fog between you and someone else. There are seven planets in your 7th House on March 11, when the empathetic Pisces New Moon makes it difficult to distinguish your feelings from someone else's—and you're likely to misread signals thanks to Mercury's retrograde on February 23–March 17. With Venus the Lover also in your 7th House on February 25–March 21, you might find yourself drawn to someone, only to discover that he or she isn't what you'd imagined. A series of planetary oppositions to perceptive Pluto in your 5th House of Romance on June 7, June 11, July 1, July 27, and August 7 creates tension, yet offers clarity. The Venus-Pluto conjunction in your 5th House on November 15 unearths intense feelings that have the power to transform your love life.

ROOM AT THE TOP

You're at the peak of your professional game with prosperous Jupiter in your 10th House of Career until June 25. In fact, the year begins on a high note with an energetic Mars-Jupiter trine in your 6th House of Work on January 4. The good news gets even better on February 6–7 as enterprising Venus and surprising Uranus align harmoniously with Jupiter, producing unexpected recognition for your hard work, boosting your self-esteem, or bringing a cash bonus. However, it's time to look farther into the future on June 25 when Jupiter shifts into your 11th House of Long-Term Goals, where it remains until July 16, 2014. Cultivate new connections within your community, develop social networks, and grow more trusting and appreciative of friends who support you.

EASY COME, EASY GO

You struggle to hold on to your cash this year with erratic Uranus in your 8th House of Investments and Shared Resources. The Libra Full Moon on March 27 illuminates your 2nd House of Finances and opposes Uranus and the money planet Venus, emphasizing your financial instability. The Libra New Moon on October 4 again opposes volatile Uranus, possibly catalyzing much-needed changes in a business relationship. The Aries Lunar Eclipse on October 18 rattles your 8th House of Joint Holdings and is another not-so-gentle reminder to keep your fiscal policy conservative right now rather than taking unnecessary risks.

LEAN ON ME

You're naturally inclined to maintain a healthy lifestyle, but you may have to learn how to ask for help when you need it this year. Chiron the Wounded Healer remains in your 7th House of Others until 2018, but trines from trustworthy Saturn on March 21 and October 2 can alleviate your fear of being vulnerable, especially if a friend comes through with the support you need. Consult a health care provider about a chronic problem around March 28–29 when interactive Mercury trines Saturn and conjuncts Chiron. Also, it's wise to increase the intensity of your workouts during macho Mars's visit to your sign on October 15–December 7.

WINDOW OF OPPORTUNITY

You'll have more fun at home—whether you're alone, with family, or with guests—when pleasurable Venus is in your 4th House of Domestic Conditions through January 8 and then again on October 7–November 5. Although you're inclined to stay close to your place of residence, Venus in high-spirited Sagittarius encourages you to turn your home into a place of adventure by hosting people from faraway places, listening to music from other cultures, or expanding your culinary skills to include other national cuisines. A boisterous Sagittarius Lunar Eclipse on May 25 shakes up your household by emboldening you to take a risk and start a remodeling project, redecorate a room, or throw a party to remember.

FLEXIBLE FLYER

You tend to travel for business purposes while opportunistic Jupiter is visiting your 10th House of Career until June 25. If possible, avoid going on a trip March 23–29 when Jupiter forms uneasy quincunxes with restrictive Saturn and formidable Pluto. Once Jupiter enters your 11th House of Friends on June 25, you're more likely to embark on an excursion for social reasons rather than for work. Even if you pay attention to every little detail when Mercury is retrograde on February 23–March 17, June 26–July 20, or October 21–November 10, prepare to make last-minute changes due to unforeseen circumstances.

GUIDING LIGHT

You are very serious about acquiring practical tools that advance your spiritual development. But study will only take you so far, even with ambitious Saturn's presence in your 3rd House of Learning. A key to your metaphysical growth is finding a teacher or guru who can take you further along the path than you could go on your own. Inspirational Neptune, making a long-term visit to your 7th House of Others, can cause you to idealize someone who seems to know more than you. Thankfully, synergetic Saturn-Neptune trines on June 11 and July 19 give you a mix of intuition and sensibility that enables you to choose a reliable guide to take you to the next level.

RICK & JEFF'S TIP FOR THE YEAR
Keep Your Eyes on the Prize

You normally prefer a more objective view of the world, so you may feel a bit disoriented with so many planets in emotional water signs this year. However, resistance to powerful waves of feelings is futile and will only bring frustration and exhaustion. Instead of fearfully holding onto the status quo, trust the wisdom of the cosmos by pushing away from the shore and into the strong currents. If you lose your bearings once you leave solid ground, the best way to prevent instability is to focus on the horizon and your future goals rather than looking back to the past.

JANUARY

POWER PLAY

You are ready to hit the ground running this month as a heightened sense of practicality enables you to express yourself methodically and advance steadily toward your goals. You're in a serious mood when your ruling planet, Mercury, in ambitious Capricorn hooks up with ruthless Pluto in your 5th House of Creativity on **January 6**, prompting you to think about getting ahead even when you're engaging in play. Valuable Venus enters calculating Capricorn and your 5th House on **January 8**, which allows you to have a good time as long as you manage to be productive, too. Since the gathering of planets in results-oriented Capricorn requires you to make a concrete plan for your success, the New Moon in the sign of the climbing Mountain Goat on the **11th** is a great time to put it into action.

The energy shifts on **January 19** as Mercury and the Sun enter conceptual Aquarius and your 6th House of Self-Improvement, giving you more freedom to adapt your daily routine to your unique way of doing business. Luckily, on **January 22–25** Mercury and the Sun form supportive aspects with innovative Uranus and fortuitous Jupiter, creating the potential for an unexpected breakthrough at work or public recognition for a job well done. These auspicious days can increase your self-confidence, which is great as long as you don't get too cocky. If you do assume that everything is copacetic, the dramatic Leo Full Moon in your 12th House of Destiny on the **26th** could be a sobering reality check as it squares karmic Saturn. The challenging Sun-Saturn square on **January 30** presents obstacles that can slow you down until you've learned your spiritual lesson.

KEEP IN MIND THIS MONTH

In the midst of all your obligations to others and commitments to yourself, schedule some playtime when you can kick back and enjoy yourself.

KEY DATES

★ **JANUARY 1–4**
lost in your mind
You're able to share your ideas more creatively
while messenger Mercury visits your 5th
House of Self-Expression. You strive to be
practical in your thinking, but a Mercury-
Neptune sextile on **January 1** infuses your
thoughts with fantasy. Although Mercury's
creative square with inventive Uranus on the
3rd can trigger intellectual brilliance, you're
not interested in conforming to other people's
expectations. Nevertheless, you're motivated
to achieve your professional objectives on
January 4, when assertive Mars in your 6th
House of Work trines far-reaching Jupiter in
your 10th House of Career.

SUPER NOVA DAYS

★ **JANUARY 7–11**
turning point
January 7 can be a rather frustrating day at
work. Impatient Mars in your 6th House of
Details squares restraining Saturn, so you

may have to wait a little longer before taking action. Fortunately, Venus enters conservative Capricorn on **January 8** and connects with spacey Neptune on the **10th**, cultivating patience as a more attractive strategy than just bolting ahead. The Capricorn New Moon on **January 11** begins a monthlong cycle of activity as it stimulates your 5th House of Love and Creativity. The New Moon's magical quintiles to brilliant Uranus and earnest Saturn bless you with an extra dose of ingenuity and charisma, emboldening you to start the next phase of your journey with renewed self-confidence.

★ **JANUARY 16-18**
you get what you need
Your emotional intensity is strong enough to heat up an intimate relationship or strengthen your resolve in a business negotiation on **January 16**, when seductive Venus joins persuasive Pluto in your 5th House of Romance and Self-Expression. You become even more determined to satisfy your desires on the **17th** when Venus supportively sextiles

persistent Saturn. Fortunately, communicator
Mercury hooks up with the radiant Sun on
the **18th** to give your words enough power to
convince others that you're speaking the truth.

★ **JANUARY 24-26**
the sky is the limit
Expect a great deal of excitement at work on
January 24 with the high-frequency electricity
of the Sun's supportive sextile to eye-opening
Uranus. The Sun's trine to expansive Jupiter
on the **25th** broadens your vision, encourages
you to set your goals higher than ever, and
instills you with enough enthusiasm to fuel a
journey to the stars. However, a methodical
Mercury-Saturn square requires you to make
certain that you've addressed all details
prior to blastoff. Your sense of invincibility
culminates with the proud Leo Full Moon on
January 26 that illuminates your 12th House of
Endings, alerting you that it's now time to slow
down and integrate the recent changes.

FEBRUARY

PERCEPTION IS REALITY

It's difficult to know what's real in your relationships this month as planets cluster in fanciful Pisces and your 7th House of Partnerships and Public Life. Your personal and professional interactions are top priority when spontaneous Mars begins the parade into your 7th House on **February 1**, followed by communicator Mercury on **February 5**, the Sun on **February 18**, and loving Venus on **February 25**. Even with this growing emphasis on others, however, you might not know where you stand with them, because each of these planets joins fuzzy Neptune after it enters Pisces, confusing your desires with reality. Excessive self-confidence can overinflate your expectations when pompous Jupiter squares Mercury on the **9th**, Mars on the **10th**, and the Sun on the **25th**. Fortunately, common sense prevails when serious Saturn trines thoughtful Mercury on the **12th** and Mars on the **16th**.

You may be more assertive than usual as your key planet, Mercury, conjuncts Mars in your interactive 7th House on **February 8**.

An uncharacteristic intensity can permeate conversations throughout the month because speedy Mercury slows down—along with your progress—until it turns retrograde on the **23rd**, tracking closely with Mars the entire time. A second Mercury-Mars conjunction on the **26th** can reactivate an old argument, even if you thought the conflict was resolved. Meanwhile, the futuristic Aquarius New Moon on **February 10** plants a seed of intention in your 6th House of Self-Improvement, encouraging you to think of new and different ways to change your everyday life for the better. The exacting Virgo Full Moon on **February 25** reminds you to pay attention to your feelings, even though practical considerations may require you to keep them to yourself to avoid conflict.

KEEP IN MIND THIS MONTH

People sometimes show up in your life to reflect issues that you need to work on. Instead of trying to fix anyone else, remember that real change starts within you.

KEY DATES

★ **FEBRUARY 5–7**
top of the world
When cerebral Mercury enters your 7th
House of Companions on **February 5**, you
shift your analytical attention from the details
of daily life to how you interact with others.
It's hard to separate your expectations from
reality, however, because Mercury joins
dreamy Neptune on **February 6**, which can be
inspiring if you remember to keep your facts
and fantasies in their proper places. You're
more willing to experiment as desirable Venus
forms a supportive sextile with unconventional
Uranus. Although you may be inclined to
try something new and different in your
relationships, Venus in your 6th House of Work
happily trines propitious Jupiter in your 10th
House of Status on the **7th**, indicating that you
could be rewarded for your ingenuity on the
job instead.

★ **FEBRUARY 10–12**
inch by inch

The quirky Aquarius New Moon on **February 10** reveals silver linings in dark clouds because it's accompanied by an upbeat Mars-Jupiter square that infuses you with excitement. But take things slowly, because severe Saturn in your 3rd House of Communication aspects Venus and Mercury on **February 11–12**, bringing delays and even setbacks if you impulsively rush ahead. Rather than wallowing in self-doubt, concentrate on what needs to be done, make a concrete plan, and then move resolutely toward your goal one step at a time.

★ **FEBRUARY 15–16**
in the zone

Warrior Mars is your ally now, gracing you with a deep reservoir of energy and the ability to collaborate effectively with others to achieve success. Mars in your 7th House of Partnerships cooperatively sextiles potent Pluto on **February 15** and trines reliable Saturn on the **16th**, empowering you to express yourself creatively while still working closely with someone else. Fortunately, your co-workers can be of great help because your high level of organization makes it easier for them to contribute their skills to the project.

SUPER NOVA DAYS

★ **FEBRUARY 23–25**
the devil is in the details
Although the hardworking Virgo Full Moon on **February 25** falls in your 1st House of Physicality, it may not be easy to accomplish your goals now. Your ruling planet, Mercury, begins its retrograde phase on **February 23** in your 7th House of Partners, possibly unraveling a working relationship. If necessary, renegotiate the details of an agreement prior to Mercury's direct turn on **March 17**. But don't push too hard for final resolution in a conflict; the Full Moon and the Sun dynamically square grandiose Jupiter, allowing you to overlook important details and possibly promise more than you can deliver.

MARCH

LOST AND FOUND

You can barely keep your thoughts distinct
from those of the people around you this
month. It's because six planets congregating
in hypersensitive Pisces and your 7th House
of Others soften the hard edges that normally
separate you from the rest of the world. A
heightened state of empathy turns your mind into
an emotional sponge, absorbing the feelings of
those closest to you. Thankfully, a long-lasting
sextile between stabilizing Saturn and surgical
Pluto on **March 8** enables you to cut through the
noise and make enduring changes to the way
you process information. However, trusting your
intuition is difficult because you naturally still
want the details, even when the psychic Pisces
New Moon on **March 11** falls in your social 7th
House.

    You're likely to misread the intentions of a
partner or misunderstand a conversation while
Mercury the Trickster is retrograde in fantasy-
prone Pisces and your 7th House of Companions
until **March 17**. You may struggle with staying
motivated because your previous goals appear

to lose some of their importance. Happily, the cobwebs of confusion begin to dissipate once clever Mercury turns direct. The pace of change picks up steam when three planets each shift into fiery Aries in your 8th House of Regeneration— Mars on the **12th**, the Sun on the **20th**, and Venus on the **21st**. But your forward motion isn't so steady on **March 23** when an anxious quincunx between optimistic Jupiter and pessimistic Saturn leaves you doubtful. The diplomatic Libra Full Moon on **March 27** brightens your 2nd House of Values, reminding you that having to make compromises doesn't mean that you must sacrifice any of your core beliefs.

KEEP IN MIND THIS MONTH

It's never easy to let go of old agendas, especially if you don't know what will replace them. Yet this step is necessary before you can start the next phase of your journey.

KEY DATES

★ **MARCH 1**
deep thoughts
You may not use many words today, but
you still get your point across succinctly.
This no-frills attitude is courtesy of the Sun
trining somber Saturn in your 3rd House of
Communication. A powerful Sun–Pluto sextile
strengthens your resolve and compels you to
express yourself creatively, even while you
fulfill your responsibilities.

★ **MARCH 4–7**
make love work
Rational Mercury's retrograde in your 7th
House of Companions is a great time to
revisit interpersonal issues, and on **March 4**
its conjunction with the Sun focuses your
thinking on relationships. Yet it's not easy
being logical as sensual Venus squares
indulgent Jupiter, increasing your desires and
encouraging you to ask for more than usual.
The topic of conversation is love when talkative
Mercury conjuncts romantic Venus on the **6th**.

Discussing difficult subjects can lead to lasting progress toward resolving your differences as Venus and Mercury trine trustworthy Saturn and sextile insightful Pluto on **March 6–7**.

★ **MARCH 9–12**
fools rush in

You say something that might be better left unsaid on **March 9**, when loquacious Mercury squares bombastic Jupiter. Although you may pause to consider other people's feelings when the compassionate Pisces New Moon lands in your 7th House of Relationships on **March 11**, you're not likely to think twice before doing something reckless when impetuous Mars blasts into dauntless Aries on **March 12**. Just remember that exercising a little caution can save the day.

★ **MARCH 20–22**
yell fire!

The Spring Equinox, marked by the Sun's move into pioneering Aries and your 8th House of Deep Sharing on **March 20**, empowers you to take a risk to increase intimacy in a relationship. Venus enters vibrant Aries on the **21st**, reinforcing your desire for an intense connection with someone special. Combustible Mars hooks up with uncontainable Uranus on the **22nd**, setting off emotional fireworks with a suitable partner or triggering a conflict if you're unhappy with your current situation.

SUPER NOVA DAYS

★ **MARCH 27–31**
navigating rough waters
You crave more harmony in your relationships with the peace-seeking Libra Full Moon on the **27th** lighting up your sociable 7th House. But the emotional currents are hard to read and you can't decide on a course of action, because aspects to adventurous Jupiter, cautious Saturn, and thrilling Uranus on **March 28–29** have you seeking stability and excitement at the same time. Uncomfortable alignments with suspicious Pluto on **March 29–31** stir up feelings of jealousy or resentment, making it difficult to relax. Nevertheless, facing these challenges can transform you into a better person if you remember to be kind and honest.

APRIL

SUSTAINABLE GROWTH

Although you begin April with a surge of progress, by midmonth the noise begins to settle down, enabling you to sustain your enthusiasm while seeking new ways to widen your horizons. Your normally cautious approach to change is at odds with the challenges you face with a cluster of planets in impulsive Aries and your 8th House of Transformation. You bring an especially creative approach to relationships on **April 6–8** when animated Mars, amorous Venus, and the Sun aspect poetic Neptune in your 7th House of Partners. The assertive Aries New Moon on the **April 10** conjuncts Mars and Venus in your 8th House, motivating you to move beyond the status quo by embracing the future rather than holding on to the past. However, resistant Saturn in your 3rd House of Immediate Environment forms an irritating quincunx with uncontrollable Uranus on **April 12**, escalating your discomfort with any transitions that are unfolding too fast. Fortunately, quicksilver Mercury dashes into trailblazing Aries on the **13th**, giving you a much-needed new perspective to handle current developments.

On **April 15** resourceful Venus enters your 9th House of Higher Thought and Faraway Places, raising your interest in subjects and activities that expand your mind and broaden your view of the world. The Sun enters dependable Taurus and your 9th House on **April 19**, followed by Mars on the **20th**, reinforcing your pragmatic approach to growth. Taskmaster Saturn's opposition to Venus on **April 22** and the Sun on **April 28** may slow your progress substantially by placing obstacles in your path, compelling you to work hard without necessarily seeing immediate gain. The enigmatic Scorpio Full Moon on **April 25** is a Lunar Eclipse that conjuncts Saturn in your 3rd House of Communication, requiring you to concentrate on one task at a time.

KEEP IN MIND THIS MONTH

Reaching your goals may depend upon your ability to turn your passion at the beginning of a project into sheer determination and willpower later on.

KEY DATES

★ **APRIL 1**
sunny-side up
It's easy to imagine that you can accomplish nearly anything today because exuberant Jupiter in your 10th House of Career and Public Life is illuminated by a supportive sextile from the Sun in fearless Aries. Others may think that you're lucky, but it's your positive attitude that's at the root of your current good fortune.

★ **APRIL 9-13**
closer to free
Mercury's magical quintile to dark Pluto on **April 9** adds depth and intensity to your messages. But when the Communicator runs into critical Saturn on the **10th**, you'll need facts to support your point of view. Tension builds as the unpremeditated Aries New Moon in your 8th House of Intimacy on the same day prompts you to reveal secrets that leave you feeling vulnerable. The conflict between sharing your emotions now and waiting for a better time is

exacerbated by Saturn's maladjusted quincunx to reckless Uranus on **April 12**. Although there may be sensible reasons to respect the confines of the current situation, Mercury's shift into headstrong Aries on the **13th** might convince you to say what's on your mind anyway.

★ **APRIL 20–23**
truth and consequences
You're compelled to express yourself—even if it will ruffle someone's feathers—when intelligent Mercury joins rebellious Uranus in your 8th House of Deep Sharing on **April 20**. Although Mars's move into steady Taurus on the same day encourages complacency, its active semisquare to opinionated Jupiter on the **21st** provokes dramatic action. Assuming that you speak your piece, an isolating Venus-Saturn opposition on **April 22** can bring harsh judgment from someone who is normally supportive. Fortunately, a cooperative Mercury-Jupiter sextile on the **23rd** helps you find the words to regain trust and earn recognition for taking an unconventional stand on an important subject.

SUPER NOVA DAYS

★ **APRIL 25–28**

practical magic

Your life feels unpredictable right now. Even
though the Sun, Venus, and Mars are all in
down-to-earth Taurus, a magnetic Scorpio
Lunar Eclipse on **April 25** in your 3rd House
of Immediate Environment infuses you with
a sense of instability. The Full Moon Eclipse
conjuncts concrete Saturn, enchanting
you with the power of your desires and the
possibility of concentrating your emotional
intensity to get what you want. Your fascination
with what lies beyond the real world is
encouraged by an illusory Mars-Neptune
sextile on the **26th**. However, the karmic Sun-
Saturn opposition on the **28th** indicates that
you won't get away with outsmarting reality if
you try to stretch it too far.

MAY

WORK IN PROGRESS

You may be frustrated by setbacks to your
plans this month, but you can rebound quickly
and establish new goals based on a deeper
awareness of who you are and how you want
to express yourself. Your ability to make long-
term plans is quite sound, with incisive Pluto in
your 5th House of Self-Expression creating a
harmonious trine with the Sun on **May 1**, Mars
on **May 5**, and Mercury on **May 7**—all in your 9th
House of Future Vision. A Taurus Solar Eclipse
in your 9th House on **May 9** is a harbinger of
unexpected change, though, even if everything
seems stable in the moment. Venus's entry into
your 10th House of Public Responsibility, also on
the **9th**, shifts your focus to seeking recognition
on the job. Your thoughts turn to more immediate
career concerns when analytical Mercury steps
into your 10th House on **May 15**. The Sun and
Mars follow suit on **May 20** and **May 31**, further
emphasizing the transition from planning for the
future to dealing with the present. All of these
planets—plus opportunistic Jupiter—traveling
through diverse Gemini may present so many

options that narrowing your focus can be problematic.

Nevertheless, bigger changes are afoot, stemming from a long-lasting square between revolutionary Uranus and evolutionary Pluto that began on **June 24, 2012**, and culminates on **March 16, 2015**. This powerful aspect is exact on **May 20**, deepening an inner conflict between your urgent need to express yourself more passionately and the growing stress it places on your personal relationships. On **May 25**, a Sagittarius Lunar Eclipse lands in your 4th House of Roots, which can put an end to unrealistic dreams about your home and family.

KEEP IN MIND THIS MONTH

Although you prefer having a concrete plan to get ahead at work, too much structure can limit your ability to adapt to changing circumstances.

KEY DATES

★ **MAY 1–5**
heroic efforts
You're ready to methodically set your strategy into motion, but may lack sufficient information as Saturn the Tester opposes Mars the Warrior in your 9th House of Big Ideas on **May 1**. Your key planet, Mercury, enters practical Taurus on the same day to help you clarify your long-range goals. Additionally, a powerful Sun-Pluto trine gives you the stamina to overcome the resistance you face. If you don't have all your facts in order, thoughtful Mercury's opposition to unforgiving Saturn on **May 5** sends you back to the drawing board until you've learned what you need to know. Again, a trine to unrelenting Pluto—this time from Mars—enables you to act on your resolve with unflappable determination.

★ **MAY 9**
lighten up
There's a sense of playfulness in the air when flirty Venus enters whimsical Gemini on **May 9**.

Yes, you're motivated to accomplish your goals, but you like the idea of having a variety of ways to reach them. The sensible Taurus New Moon Eclipse reminds you that the simplest approach is still the best one, while cautioning you against becoming so stuck in your ways that you lose your ability to adapt to the big changes coming your way.

SUPER NOVA DAYS

★ **MAY 18-20**
tricky currents

While you're great at analyzing a situation to make a smart decision, Virgo, a lot of uncertainty is packed into these days. Brainy Mercury is in your 10th House of Status and its square to deceptive Neptune on **May 18** can be confusing if you're under pressure to make an immediate choice, especially when others are depending on you to lead the way. An unorthodox Venus-Uranus sextile encourages you to try a new route to reach your destination, and Mercury's sextile to Uranus on the **20th** is ready to reward your originality. Yet all your well-intended efforts

may be for naught in light of large-scale social
changes that stem from the life-changing
Uranus-Pluto square that's exact on **May 20**.

★ **MAY 25–28**
   the time to hesitate is through
   Just as you begin to gain traction, a confusing
   Sun-Neptune square on the **26th** starts you
   wondering whether or not you're heading in
   the right direction. Thankfully, any self-doubt
   quickly dissipates when Mercury and Venus
   conjunct sanguine Jupiter, inspiring you with
   new ideas and a greater sense of worth on
   May 27–28. Don't be afraid to take a risk—as
   long as you bring along some of your famous
   common sense.

JUNE

THE PERSISTENCE OF ILLUSION

The pressure for change doesn't let up this
month, but you will have days when your
uncertainty vanishes and even the most fleeting
dreams appear vividly real. These moments,
however brief, are not meant to confuse you;
rather, they are opportunities to make your
wishes come true. Industrious Saturn in your 3rd
House of Data Collection forms a trine to elusive
Neptune in your 7th House of Partnerships on
June 11, empowering you to build new structures
that support your vision, ground your intuition,
and sharpen your instincts in business and
personal relationships. However, this Saturn-
Neptune trine is strengthened on **June 3** when
cunning Mercury creates a stabilizing Grand
Water Trine with these two slow-moving planets,
enabling you to make a concrete plan that can
stand the test of time. On **June 7**, glamorous
Venus follows the pattern to trine Saturn and
Neptune, enhancing the possibilities before you
while giving you the patience and follow-through
to see your aspirations materialize. It's the
radiant Sun's turn to illuminate and crystallize

your opportunities when it completes the grand trine on **June 26**, sustaining this constructive pattern throughout the month.

Meanwhile, you're eager to seek recognition in your chosen field thanks to the restless Gemini New Moon on **June 8** that emphasizes your 10th House of Career and Responsibility. The earthy Capricorn Full Moon on **June 23** lands in your 5th House of Self-Expression, encouraging you to carve out some time for creative endeavors and enjoy playtime with your inner child or the children in your world. Mercury's retrograde turn in your 11th House of Pals on **June 26** begins a three-week period of introspection, prompting you to review recent social events, reevaluate your role in organizations, and rethink your goals for the rest of the year.

KEEP IN MIND THIS MONTH

You can minimize the stress associated with big changes by focusing your attention on a single goal and relentlessly keeping your eyes on the prize.

KEY DATES

★ **JUNE 2–3**

you've got a friend

You long to cultivate more nurturing relationships when lovable Venus meanders into sensitive Cancer and your 11th House of Friends and Associates on **June 2**. You could greatly benefit from participating in a group activity when interactive Mercury, also in your 11th House, forms a Grand Water Trine with Saturn and Neptune on **June 3**. Although you may be tempted to keep your feelings to yourself, sharing them can lead to increased relationship stability in your everyday life.

SUPER NOVA DAYS

★ **JUNE 7–8**

embrace the unknown

There is more going on than meets the eye when curious Mercury opposes secretive Pluto on **June 7** and squares shocking Uranus on the **8th**, creating some excitement and turmoil. However, procrastination abounds when forceful Mars squares confusing

Neptune on the **7th**, dissipating your energy and reducing your ability to take decisive action. Happily, you feel loved by your friends as appreciative Venus in your 11th House of Community harmonizes with enduring Saturn and idealistic Neptune. The adaptable Gemini New Moon on **June 8** showcases your ability to move back and forth between stressful periods of uncertainty and relaxing moments of peaceful coexistence.

★ **JUNE 11–15**
building a mystery
Needy Venus opposes punishing Pluto on **June 11** and squares volatile Uranus on the **12th**, fomenting emotional conflict that can make romance feel like a battlefield. But a powerful trine between solid Saturn and surreal Neptune on the **11th** enables you to ground even your most unrealistic ideas. On **June 14**, a snappy Sun-Uranus quintile activates your inner nerd and sparks flashes of ingenuity that move you closer to your goals. However, a crunchy Mars-Pluto quincunx on the **15th** can stymie your

progress toward your objectives, especially
if you mistakenly think that manipulative
behavior will take you where you want to go.

★ **JUNE 19–23**
simply irresistible
You may see opportunity everywhere you look
on **June 19** when the Sun conjuncts cheerful
Jupiter in your 10th House of Career. You are
extraordinarily persuasive and can sweet-talk
your way into someone's heart on the **20th**
as chatty Mercury hooks up with charming
Venus. The Sun's entry into self-protective
Cancer and your 11th House of Groups on
June 21 marks the Summer Solstice, a time
when your friends and associates assume
an increasingly important role in your life.
However, the crafty Capricorn Full Moon in
your 5th House of Love on **June 23** reveals
emotions that test the boundaries separating
a romance from a friendship.

JULY

FIELD OF DREAMS

Explore the outer limits this month by imagining the possibilities ahead rather than solely focusing on concrete objectives. The planetary gathering in your 11th House of Long-Term Goals inspires you to seek the pot of gold at rainbow's end, even if you don't know how to get there just yet. You're likely to reexamine old expectations before thinking about your new mission as your ruling planet, Mercury, retrogrades through reflective Cancer and your 11th House until **July 20**. State your intentions as clearly as possible on **July 8** when the caring Cancer New Moon, also in your 11th House, invites you to plant a seed of intention that you can nurture to fruition over the weeks ahead.

Fortunately, you can easily crystallize the best parts of your diaphanous visions because of a long-lasting holding pattern between disciplined Saturn in resourceful Scorpio and magical Neptune in creative Pisces. This Saturn-Neptune trine is exact on **July 19** and is the final occurrence of a series that began on **October 10, 2012**, empowering you to manifest your dreams. Luckily, bountiful Jupiter and competent Mars trine Saturn and Neptune on **July 17** and **July 20**, helping to make your wishes come true. This consolidating Grand Water Trine reminds you that steady progress is possible and allows you to integrate a deeper spiritual perspective into your life. On **July 22**, a boisterous Mars-Jupiter conjunction in your futuristic 11th House raises your confidence and increases your zest, motivating you to strive for perfection. However, Venus's shift into discerning Virgo, along with an intelligent Aquarius Full Moon that brightens your 6th House of Details, place you on familiar ground and remind you that working smarter is better than working harder.

KEEP IN MIND THIS MONTH

Don't just rely on your sharp perceptions and cool logic; try sinking into your feelings and letting intuition be your guide.

KEY DATES

★ **JULY 1**

against all odds

You may feel deprived of emotional satisfaction on **July 1** when Venus squares Saturn in your 3rd House of Communication. Trying to build bridges just creates frustration; the gulf between you and others only seems to widen. Suffering is tough, especially when an unflinching Sun-Pluto opposition adds tension to the mix. An unrealistic Venus-Neptune quincunx may encourage escapist behavior, but resolution is hidden in the storm clouds if you're brave enough to penetrate the fog.

★ **JULY 4–7**

free bird

Your rebellious behavior puts others on notice that you're not willing to play by their arbitrary rules on **July 4**, when the Sun in defensive Cancer dynamically squares Uranus in disruptive Aries. This electric combo allows you to see things differently, but you might lose objectivity when mental Mercury runs into fuzzy

Neptune the next day, distracting you from your tasks and prompting absentmindedness. You're attracted to the unusual as lovely Venus conspires with quirky Uranus in your 8th House of Intimacy and Shared Resources on the **7th**. Instead of clinging to past memories, find exhilaration in recognizing that you're emotionally free to express your true desires.

SUPER NOVA DAYS

★ **JULY 17–20**

the power of now

Your imagination expands on **July 17** when philosophical Jupiter harmoniously aligns with planetary heavyweights Saturn and Neptune, and then you receive a blast of assertive energy as warrior Mars marches into the picture on **July 20**. Saturn adds realism to transcendent Neptune and hopeful Jupiter, inspiring practical speculation and authentic altruism. Mercury's direct turn on the **20th** is another signal to start working on a new project. Although your creativity may be off the charts, ultimately it is your patient perseverance that ensures enduring success.

★ **JULY 22**
adrenaline rush
Action-hero Mars and jovial Jupiter meet up
today, turning you into an enthusiastic dynamo
of energy. If you can't channel your excitement
into creative activities, at least go to the gym
and work some of it off. The eclectic Aquarius
Full Moon illuminates your 6th House of Self-
Improvement, offering you an opportunity to
balance your fastidious attention to details
with a more lighthearted approach.

★ **JULY 27**
dangerous curves ahead
Pessimism or fear can alter your perceptions
on **July 27** when contentious Mars in your
11th House of Social Networking opposes
underhanded Pluto, making it hard to
know who's on your team and who may be
undermining your work. Additionally, a critical
Sun-Saturn square can weigh you down with
responsibility. Don't be discouraged; drive
carefully and wait until the road straightens
out before resuming your speed.

AUGUST

THE SHOW MUST GO ON

This month of exciting opportunities comes when you're ready to push hard for success—and it's appropriate to establish new behaviors that help you to realize your dreams. Just don't waste your energy filling in too many details of your action plan; there will be many surprising twists and turns along the way. Being flexible may be as important now as being prepared. Overblown Jupiter, moving through your 11th House of Long-Term Goals, is a significant player as it opposes scheming Pluto on **August 7** and squares radical Uranus on **August 21**. You may feel as if Easy Street is just around the next corner, tempting you to take a shortcut and make a mad dash for the finish line. Unfortunately, this is not a wise strategy—opposing forces may be stronger than you realize. Proceed with caution instead of trying to take advantage of every situation and force progress before its time.

Meanwhile, you're torn between expression and silence. The Sun is shining in dramatic Leo until **August 22**, urging you to share what's in your heart. However, the showy Leo Sun is hiding out in your 12th House of Privacy, so your shyness or humility could make you reluctant to say what you feel. You may worry about what others think of you or feel nervous about speaking in front of a group on **August 6**, when the theatrical Leo New Moon activates your quiet 12th House. The eccentric Aquarius Full Moon on **August 20** illuminates your 6th House of Self-Improvement, opening your mind to new ways of handling your daily routine.

KEEP IN MIND THIS MONTH

When you make decisions by rationally eliminating unrealistic choices, you limit your options. Instead, try entertaining each possibility on its own merits as it appears.

KEY DATES

★ **AUGUST 1–4**
playing on the edge
You struggle to decide what you want on
August 1, when a difficult Sun-Pluto quincunx
lowers your vitality but a jumpy Venus-
Uranus aspect provokes you to take a risk.
Independent Uranus in your 8th House of
Deep Sharing exacerbates the contradiction
between your yearning for affection and your
search for freedom. However, the cosmic
lovers ignite passion as feminine Venus
and masculine Mars seductively dance on
August 2. A thrilling Sun-Uranus trine on
August 4 opens doors that were previously
locked, but it's still up to you to take advantage
of the more permissive environment.

★ **AUGUST 7**
top dog
You want to stretch the envelope with your
big ideas now that giant Jupiter in your 11th
House of Goals opposes powerful Pluto. You
may feel ten feet tall and bulletproof with

a strong desire to control other people—or at least strongly influence them. But if you are too forceful today, some unexpected consequences will soon need your attention.

★ **AUGUST 11–14**
every cloud has a silver lining
You doubt yourself after an encounter with a hypercritical person thanks to Mercury's square to sobering Saturn on **August 11**. Unfortunately, it's easy to get stuck in a negative mental groove on **August 13**, when compulsive Pluto irritates overanalytical Mercury in your 12th House of Spirituality. However, despair is short-lived because Mercury's fluid trine to ingenious Uranus on **August 14** hands you the keys of innovation that let you escape from your self-designed box.

SUPER NOVA DAYS

★ **AUGUST 20–23**
anything goes
You're sure that you can achieve unrealistic goals if you just make enough plans on

August 20, when the radical Aquarius Full
Moon highlights your 6th House of Details.
The next day, though, a jolting Jupiter-Uranus
square blasts open a window of opportunity
that suddenly reveals a variety of new options.
On **August 22**, witty Mercury aligns with Jupiter
and Uranus, sparking even more creative
thoughts, so take the time to write down your
inspirations before they fade. Thankfully, the
Sun enters methodical Virgo on the **22nd**,
followed by Mercury on the **23rd**, enabling you
to put your best ideas to practical use.

★ **AUGUST 26–27**
shake, rattle, and roll
You're ready to do something totally different
on **August 26** when a titillating Venus-Uranus
opposition awakens unusual interests, yet a
bewildering Sun-Neptune opposition in your
relationship houses adds confusion and chaos
to the mix. Still, a quick departure from the
norm will do wonders for your psyche. Just
make sure you don't overdo it; an indulgent
Venus-Jupiter square on **August 27** can tempt
you with excess.

SEPTEMBER

SHINE YOUR LIGHT

You're eager to show others how competent you are with the bright Sun in your efficient sign and your 1st House of Self until **September 22.** Thankfully, you can express yourself clearly with your ruling planet, Mercury, also in precise Virgo until **September 9.** The problem is that sometimes you might as well be pushing a boulder up a steep hill, while at other times circumstances move so quickly you can't keep up with them. A number of awkward quincunxes throughout the month—on the **2nd, 3rd, 11th, 20th, and 25th**—make it difficult to find your groove and sustain a steady pace of progress. But positive aspects to beneficial Jupiter in your 11th House of Goals on **September 7, 21, and 26** suggest that your current efforts will pay off if you worry less about your day-to-day accomplishments and just focus on your ultimate destination.

The analytical Virgo New Moon on **September 5** lands in your physical 1st House, and its supportive sextile from effusive Jupiter gives you an extra boost of energy. However, the Moon's anxious quincunx with irrepressible Uranus in your 8th House of Shared Resources can trigger an unexpected disagreement with a close friend or business partner. Mercury's entry into fair-minded Libra and your 2nd House of Self-Worth on **September 9** enables you to discuss your needs objectively and make compromises without lowering your self-esteem. Your attention shifts toward the needs of others on **September 19**, when the empathetic Pisces Full Moon brightens your 7th House of Partnerships. The Sun's shift into diplomatic Libra and your 2nd House of Values marks the Autumn Equinox on **September 22**, reminding you to be fair and gentle when you criticize yourself or others.

KEEP IN MIND THIS MONTH

Although it may feel as if you're spending a lot of time putting out fires, you're actually making more progress than you realize.

KEY DATES

★ **SEPTEMBER 1–3**
destination unknown
Because you understand how to express your
personal power and creativity, you can have a
profound impact on others by simply showing
up and being yourself. On **September 1**, the
willful Sun in your 1st House of Self forms a
trine with mysterious Pluto in your 5th House
of Romance, enabling you to make a lasting
impression on someone you admire. However,
you could lose focus when fearless Mars
aligns with foggy Neptune on **September 2**.
Adjust your course of action as necessary
when the Sun forms an uneasy quincunx
to erratic Uranus on the **3rd**. Instead of
having a rigid plan, prepare to make minor
modifications as necessary as you travel.

SUPER NOVA DAYS

★ **SEPTEMBER 5–9**
cool your jets
Focus your attention on practical matters
during the earthy Virgo New Moon on

September 5. Your precise concentration fades, your horizons expand, and you begin to entertain alternative strategies on **September 7**, as the Sun sextiles visionary Jupiter in your 11th House of Dreams and Wishes. Rational thinking gives way to a rising tide of desires on the **8th**, when sensual Venus forms a creative quintile with provocative Pluto. You might try to restore emotional balance when Mercury enters objective Libra on the **9th**, but hot Mars's stressful square to cold Saturn forces you to slam on the brakes. You haven't run into a wall; this is simply a reminder for you to pay attention to external conditions and not just your inner needs.

★ **SEPTEMBER 16–19**
no escape
Your thoughts are unconstrained by reason when quicksilver Mercury opposes electric Uranus on **September 16** and squares effervescent Jupiter on the **19th**. But you still may feel isolated or undeserving of love on the **18th** when receptive Venus joins doubting Saturn in your 3rd House of Communication.

You may have to control your feelings, but you still must deal with other people's emotional dramas precipitated by the hypersensitive Pisces Full Moon on the **19th**, illuminating your 7th House of Companions.

★ **SEPTEMBER 26–28**
on a wing and a prayer
All is well on **September 26** as enchanting Venus harmonizes with auspicious Jupiter, enabling you to see beauty and opportunity everywhere you look. An edgy Venus-Mars square on the **28th** can fuel a lovers' spat or a sexy encounter. Either way, Jupiter's alignment with bewitching Neptune in your 7th House of Relationships places your fantasies in the pilot's seat, revealing the infinite possibilities of an unobstructed, cloudless sky.

OCTOBER

CHASING THE BOTTOM LINE

Your finances are your primary concern this month as the Libra Sun moves through your 2nd House of Money until **October 23**. The Sun's stressful aspects with heavy-handed Pluto on **October 1** and unpredictable Uranus on **October 3** can catch you off guard and send you scrambling to get your cash flow back under control. Problems with a business partner may be disruptive during the normally even-tempered Libra New Moon on **October 4** as it opposes Uranus in your 8th House of Shared Resources. You would really like to establish stability in your daily affairs, but when steady Saturn forms an anxious quincunx with chaotic Uranus on **October 5**, you can't seem to regain a sense of order no matter how hard you try. This unstable connection with Uranus is reactivated by mischievous Mercury on **October 8** and **November 1**, yet you're more serious when the Winged Messenger conjuncts Saturn on **October 29**, prompting you to focus on the details that will ultimately make or break your plans.

Action-hero Mars rushes into your 1st House

of Self on **October 15**, heating up your sign and
pushing you to be more assertive than usual.
It's time to take charge, define your boundaries,
and defend them against anyone who might try
to boss you around. But staying centered can be
challenging now, especially around the reckless
Aries Full Moon Eclipse on **October 18** that zaps
your 2nd and 8th Houses of Resources, evoking
contradictory feelings about your personal
core values, what you own, and what you share.
Gaining clarity isn't easy when Mars opposes
dreamy Neptune on **October 19** and thoughtful
Mercury begins its three-week retrograde cycle
on **October 21**.

KEEP IN MIND THIS MONTH

*Be patient with yourself if your priorities seem to
change as you get closer to making a major decision.
Reconsider what's negotiable and what's not.*

KEY DATES

★ **OCTOBER 1–4**
stand up for your rights

An inspirational person motivates you to take the high road as communicator Mercury forms a fluid trine with spiritual Neptune in your 7th House of Others on **October 1**. Don't let your idealism turn into escapist behavior, though, because someone may be testing your ability to defend yourself when unyielding Pluto squares the Sun in your 2nd House of Values. A conflict can grow out of hand by **October 3** as the Sun opposes wild Uranus. An extreme position won't lead to a resolution, so use the diplomacy skills of the peace-keeping Libra New Moon on the **4th** to find middle ground.

★ **OCTOBER 10–12**
who's on first?

You're so confused that you don't even know who is pulling the strings when Venus and the Sun create critical aspects to dizzy Neptune in your 7th House of Companions on **October 10**.

You're tempted to overreact or turn a molehill into a mountain on **October 11–12** as Venus and the Sun are stressed by overbearing Jupiter. Things are neither as bad nor as good as they seem. Trying to force an answer to an unclear question will only make matters worse, so let the energy settle back down on its own instead.

★ **OCTOBER 16–19**
call of the wild
You're ready to step outside the box and try something completely new and different on **October 16**, thanks to a trine between pleasure-seeking Venus and unconventional Uranus. On **October 18**, the impetuous Aries Full Moon Eclipse lands in your 8th House of Intimacy, provoking you to take a risk by expressing your innermost feelings without thinking about the consequences. But exercise a little self-restraint and self-reflection, because independent Mars opposes intoxicating Neptune on the **19th**, possibly muddling your actions. You may think you know where you're heading, but your actions

may not reflect your intentions; proceed with
extreme caution.

SUPER NOVA DAYS

★ **OCTOBER 29–31**
  the buck stops here
  You've been reviewing your plans since your
  ruling planet, Mercury, turned retrograde on
  October 21; now it's time to apply what you've
  learned. On **October 29**, Mercury's conjunction
  with authoritative Saturn in your 3rd House of
  Communication demands that you say what
  you mean and mean what you say. There's
  very little margin for error, so decide what
  makes the most sense and then be precise
  as you inform others of your choice. A potent
  Mars-Pluto trine fortifies your actions on the
  31st, but don't be too aggressive or wild and
  crazy Uranus will undo the gains you've made.

NOVEMBER

LEARNING TO FLY

Your relationship to the children in your world and to your own playful spirit is in the midst of a deep and lasting shift as revolutionary Uranus forms a dynamic square to evolutionary Pluto in your 5th House of Fun. Although this powerful aspect—the fourth in a series that began on **June 24, 2012**, and finishes on **March 16, 2015**—is exact on **November 1**, expect personal and business interactions to be stressed throughout the month as you weigh what you want against what you can realistically expect. On **November 14–15**, charming Venus squares unbridled Uranus and joins passionate Pluto in your 8th House of Deep Sharing, intensifying your desires and prompting reckless behavior. Make a plan and stick with it, even if it requires all your discipline and self-restraint, especially when the Scorpio Solar Eclipse conjuncts exacting Saturn in your 3rd House of Communication on **November 3**. You might even receive a bit of help from trickster Mercury—retrograde in your 3rd House until **November 10**—requiring you to reprioritize your daily schedule so you can be even more efficient once it turns direct.

Later in the month you're eager to widen your horizons and open your mind to new experiences when the Taurus Full Moon on **November 17** lights up your 9th House of Travel and Education. At the same time, the Moon's harsh aspects to Uranus and Pluto reactivate an unresolved interpersonal conflict from earlier this month, making it more difficult for you to spread your wings. Although the Sun's entry into adventurous Sagittarius on **November 21** gives you the confidence to set lofty goals, Mercury's conjunction with stern Saturn on **November 25** slows you down long enough to make sure that you have all your facts straight before continuing on your way.

KEEP IN MIND THIS MONTH

There is a more serious side to play that allows you to explore your creativity productively while also having fun.

KEY DATES

SUPER NOVA DAYS

★ **NOVEMBER 1–3**

now or never

Sudden changes in a relationship take you by surprise and send you back to the drawing board to figure out a new game plan as shocking Uranus squares purging Pluto on **November 1**. Fortunately, expressive Mercury helps you switch up your strategy—if you're willing to say what's on your mind. Mercury is retrograde now, encouraging you to look back and reconsider your expectations. Its conjunction with the investigative Scorpio Sun in your 3rd House of Immediate Environment motivates you to dig beneath the surface to get to the core of what's going on. Initiating a difficult conversation can clear the air of negativity and permit you to move ahead in the following weeks. The Scorpio Solar Eclipse on **November 3** acts as a point of no return, thrusting you forward whether you're ready or not.

★ **NOVEMBER 8–12**
smooth operator
A sparkling Mercury-Venus sextile on
November 8 helps you to turn on the charm,
while a hardworking Mars-Saturn sextile on
the **9th** gives you the energy to finish whatever
project you start. Thankfully, recent planning
will soon begin to pay off as enterprising
Mercury turns direct on **November 10**. Your
chances for success are greatly improved
on **November 12** by the Sun's lucky trine to
abundant Jupiter in your 11th House of Goals.

★ **NOVEMBER 17–20**
great expectations
On **November 17**, the Taurus Full Moon
brightens your 9th House of Big Ideas,
suggesting that you could improve your
prospects for advancement by enrolling
in a course of study. Self-directed Mars in
your sign forms a cooperative sextile with
propitious Jupiter on the **19th**, inspiring you
to reach higher than ever before. Although
Mercury's crunchy quincunx to edgy Uranus
on the **20th** nudges you to share your ideas

before they're fully developed, its sextile to
unrelenting Pluto gives you the determination
to keep trying until you get it right.

★ **NOVEMBER 27–30**
too clever for your own good
You can communicate your ideas with ease on
November 27–28, when gregarious Mercury in
your 3rd House of Information forms positive
aspects to friendly Venus and confident
Jupiter. But an overindulgent Venus-Jupiter
opposition on the **28th** entices you to focus
only on the good stuff, which can make others
question your motives. Although an ingenious
Sun-Uranus trine makes you sound smart
on the **30th**, an annoying Mercury-Uranus
alignment means that others may not be able
to understand what you're saying unless you
simplify your concept and explain everything
very carefully.

DECEMBER

NO REST FOR THE WEARY

The theme of home and family looms large this holiday month, which begins with an inspirational Sagittarius New Moon on **December 2**, activating your 4th House of Foundations. Friendly Mercury enters forward-looking Sagittarius on **December 4**, motivating you to think ahead and make plans to enjoy this special season with those you love. Reckless Mars shifts into logical Libra and your 2nd House of Money on **December 7**, requiring you to maintain a balanced approach to your finances when considering your upcoming expenses. Fortunately, on **December 12** an ambitious Saturn-Jupiter trine offers you an opportunity to reach your goals if you're willing to restrict your personal time so you can work unencumbered by distractions.

The dualistic Gemini Full Moon on **December 17** illuminates your 10th House of Career, encouraging you to keep your options open at work. Although an unrestrained Jupiter-Neptune alignment allows you to see possibilities you might normally miss, it can be difficult to choose one path when you have so many alternatives. The

Sun's entry into traditional Capricorn and your 5th House of Fun and Games on **December 21**—the Winter Solstice—favors you with a keen sense of organization, especially when celebrations are involved. However, loving Venus turns retrograde the same day, initiating an emotional cycle of delayed satisfaction that lasts until **January 31, 2014**. Don't let your frustration turn into a temper tantrum when angry Mars opposes volatile Uranus on **December 25** and squares unforgiving Pluto on **December 30**. Rational Mercury creates stressful alignments with Uranus, Pluto, and Mars on **December 29–31**, setting the stage for a tumultuous end of the year. Your willingness to communicate honestly without blaming others turns a chaotic time into an exciting New Year's Eve.

KEEP IN MIND THIS MONTH

You won't have to travel to some exotic place to bring a little fun and adventure into your life. You can enjoy the best times while staying right at home.

KEY DATES

★ **DECEMBER 1–3**
light at the end of the tunnel
You may have trouble sleeping on **December 1**
when an anxious Mercury-Pluto semisquare
keeps you awake. You could hopelessly spin
your mental wheels, trying to figure out a way
around an unpleasant situation. Thankfully,
the visionary Sagittarius New Moon on
December 2 broadens your perspective
to discover a solution to a long-standing
problem. Trust your intuition; an otherworldly
Mercury-Mars sextile on the **3rd** will lead you
in the right direction.

★ **DECEMBER 10–12**
time is on your side
Your mind lights up on **December 10** as
Mercury in exuberant Sagittarius creates
a superconductive trine with explosive
Uranus. Although you can figure out how
to get what you want now, your impatience
creates problems if others can't keep up with
your lightning-fast thinking. Luckily, your

persistence elicits the support you need from friends and associates when generous Jupiter in your 11th House of Community trines steadfast Saturn on the **12th**.

★ **DECEMBER 16–17**
curb your enthusiasm
You might say too much about a family matter when gossipy Mercury in your domestic 4th House quincunxes excessive Jupiter on **December 16**. The flighty Gemini Full Moon on **December 17** makes it tough to get much accomplished if you're scattering your energy by trying to do too many things at once. Finally, a dynamic sesquisquare between Jupiter and nebulous Neptune makes it a challenge to bring your dreams down to earth. Nevertheless, consciously focusing on one task at a time is an antidote to haphazardly mismanaging your calendar.

★ **DECEMBER 24–25**
a house of cards
Relationships take an unexpected twist, but Mercury's shift into conservative Capricorn

and your 5th House of Spontaneity on
December 24 should help you manage
it. However, an irrepressible Mars-
Uranus opposition on **December 25** can
bring a thrilling surprise—or a sudden
disappointment. Be adaptable and prepare to
change your plans at a moment's notice.

SUPER NOVA DAYS

★ **DECEMBER 29–31**

give peace a chance

Your self-esteem is tested as Mars in your
2nd House of Self-Worth forms a difficult
square with ruthless Pluto on **December 30**.
The Sun and Mercury bring additional stress
on **December 29–31** when they cross paths
with Pluto and Uranus, provoking you to
stand up for your beliefs even against great
odds. Don't let your emotions get the best
of you, or you may say or do something
you'll later regret. Fortunately, the Sun and
Mercury sextile Chiron the Wounded Healer
on **December 30–31**, teaching you that
forgiveness is all that's truly important now.

APPENDIXES

★

2013 MONTH-AT-A-GLANCE ASTROCALENDAR

★

FAMOUS VIRGOS

★

VIRGO IN LOVE

TUESDAY 1 ★ You're motivated to achieve your professional objectives

WEDNESDAY 2 ★

THURSDAY 3 ★

FRIDAY 4 ★

SATURDAY 5

SUNDAY 6

MONDAY 7 ★ **SUPER NOVA DAYS** Wait a little longer before taking action

TUESDAY 8 ★

WEDNESDAY 9 ★

THURSDAY 10 ★

FRIDAY 11 ★ ●

SATURDAY 12

SUNDAY 13

MONDAY 14

TUESDAY 15

WEDNESDAY 16 ★ A boost of emotional intensity heats up a relationship

THURSDAY 17 ★

FRIDAY 18 ★

SATURDAY 19

SUNDAY 20

MONDAY 21

TUESDAY 22

WEDNESDAY 23

THURSDAY 24 ★ Set your goals higher than ever

FRIDAY 25 ★

SATURDAY 26 ★ ○

SUNDAY 27

MONDAY 28

TUESDAY 29

WEDNESDAY 30

THURSDAY 31

★ designates key date

FRIDAY 1

SATURDAY 2

SUNDAY 3

MONDAY 4

TUESDAY 5 ★ Keep your facts and fantasies in their proper places

WEDNESDAY 6 ★

THURSDAY 7 ★

FRIDAY 8

SATURDAY 9

SUNDAY 10 ★ ● Move resolutely toward your goal one step at a time

MONDAY 11 ★

TUESDAY 12 ★

WEDNESDAY 13

THURSDAY 14

FRIDAY 15 ★ Collaborate with others to achieve success

SATURDAY 16 ★

SUNDAY 17

MONDAY 18

TUESDAY 19

WEDNESDAY 20

THURSDAY 21

FRIDAY 22

SATURDAY 23 ★ SUPER NOVA DAYS Don't promise more than you can deliver

SUNDAY 24 ★

MONDAY 25 ★ ○

TUESDAY 26

WEDNESDAY 27

THURSDAY 28

FRIDAY 1 ★ Express yourself creatively

SATURDAY 2

SUNDAY 3

MONDAY 4 ★ The topic of conversation is love

TUESDAY 5 ★

WEDNESDAY 6 ★

THURSDAY 7 ★

FRIDAY 8

SATURDAY 9 ★ Exercising a little caution can save the day

SUNDAY 10 ★

MONDAY 11 ★ ●

TUESDAY 12 ★

WEDNESDAY 13

THURSDAY 14

FRIDAY 15

SATURDAY 16

SUNDAY 17

MONDAY 18

TUESDAY 19

WEDNESDAY 20 ★ Take a risk in a meaningful relationship

THURSDAY 21 ★

FRIDAY 22 ★

SATURDAY 23

SUNDAY 24

MONDAY 25

TUESDAY 26

WEDNESDAY 27 ★ ○ SUPER NOVA DAYS The emotional currents are hard to read

THURSDAY 28 ★

FRIDAY 29 ★

SATURDAY 30 ★

SUNDAY 31 ★

MONDAY 1 ★ Your positive attitude creates good fortune

TUESDAY 2

WEDNESDAY 3

THURSDAY 4

FRIDAY 5

SATURDAY 6

SUNDAY 7

MONDAY 8

TUESDAY 9 ★ Say what's on your mind

WEDNESDAY 10 ★ ●

THURSDAY 11 ★

FRIDAY 12 ★

SATURDAY 13 ★

SUNDAY 14

MONDAY 15

TUESDAY 16

WEDNESDAY 17

THURSDAY 18

FRIDAY 19

SATURDAY 20 ★ Expressing yourself becomes more urgent

SUNDAY 21 ★

MONDAY 22 ★

TUESDAY 23 ★

WEDNESDAY 24

THURSDAY 25 ★ ○ **SUPER NOVA DAYS** Don't try to outsmart reality

---

FRIDAY 26 ★

SATURDAY 27 ★

SUNDAY 28 ★

MONDAY 29

TUESDAY 30

WEDNESDAY 1 ★ Clarify your long-range goals

THURSDAY 2 ★

FRIDAY 3 ★

SATURDAY 4 ★

SUNDAY 5 ★

MONDAY 6

TUESDAY 7

WEDNESDAY 8

THURSDAY 9 ★ ● There's a sense of playfulness in the air

FRIDAY 10

SATURDAY 11

SUNDAY 12

MONDAY 13

TUESDAY 14

WEDNESDAY 15

THURSDAY 16

FRIDAY 17

SATURDAY 18 ★ **SUPER NOVA DAYS** Try a new route to reach your destination

---

SUNDAY 19 ★

MONDAY 20 ★

TUESDAY 21

WEDNESDAY 22

THURSDAY 23

FRIDAY 24

SATURDAY 25 ★ ○ Don't be afraid to take a risk

SUNDAY 26 ★

MONDAY 27 ★

TUESDAY 28 ★

WEDNESDAY 29

THURSDAY 30

FRIDAY 31

SATURDAY 1

SUNDAY 2 ★ Cultivate more nurturing relationships

MONDAY 3 ★

TUESDAY 4

WEDNESDAY 5

THURSDAY 6

FRIDAY 7 ★ **SUPER NOVA DAYS** There is more going on than meets the eye

SATURDAY 8 ★ ●

SUNDAY 9

MONDAY 10

TUESDAY 11 ★ Activate your inner genius

WEDNESDAY 12 ★

THURSDAY 13 ★

FRIDAY 14 ★

SATURDAY 15 ★

SUNDAY 16

MONDAY 17

TUESDAY 18

WEDNESDAY 19 ★ You can sweet talk your way into someone's heart

THURSDAY 20 ★

FRIDAY 21 ★

SATURDAY 22 ★

SUNDAY 23 ★ ○

MONDAY 24

TUESDAY 25

WEDNESDAY 26

THURSDAY 27

FRIDAY 28

SATURDAY 29

SUNDAY 30

MONDAY 1 ★ Attempts to build bridges could create frustration

TUESDAY 2

WEDNESDAY 3

THURSDAY 4 ★ You're attracted to the unusual now

FRIDAY 5 ★

SATURDAY 6 ★

SUNDAY 7 ★

MONDAY 8 ●

TUESDAY 9

WEDNESDAY 10

THURSDAY 11

FRIDAY 12

SATURDAY 13

SUNDAY 14

MONDAY 15

TUESDAY 16

WEDNESDAY 17 ★ SUPER NOVA DAYS Patient perseverance ensures success

THURSDAY 18 ★

FRIDAY 19 ★

SATURDAY 20 ★

SUNDAY 21

MONDAY 22 ★ O Channel your excitement into creative activities

TUESDAY 23

WEDNESDAY 24

THURSDAY 25

FRIDAY 26

SATURDAY 27 ★ Pessimism or fear can alter your perceptions

SUNDAY 28

MONDAY 29

TUESDAY 30

WEDNESDAY 31

THURSDAY 1 ★ You may have difficulty deciding what you want

FRIDAY 2 ★

SATURDAY 3 ★

SUNDAY 4 ★

MONDAY 5

TUESDAY 6 ●

WEDNESDAY 7 ★ Stretch the envelope

THURSDAY 8

FRIDAY 9

SATURDAY 10

SUNDAY 11 ★ Every cloud has a silver lining

MONDAY 12 ★

TUESDAY 13 ★

WEDNESDAY 14 ★

THURSDAY 15

FRIDAY 16

SATURDAY 17

SUNDAY 18

MONDAY 19

TUESDAY 20 ★ ○ **SUPER NOVA DAYS** Put your best ideas to practical use

WEDNESDAY 21 ★

THURSDAY 22 ★

FRIDAY 23 ★

SATURDAY 24

SUNDAY 25

MONDAY 26 ★ A departure from the norm will do wonders for your psyche

TUESDAY 27 ★

WEDNESDAY 28

THURSDAY 29

FRIDAY 30

SATURDAY 31

SUNDAY 1 ★ Adjust your course of action as necessary

MONDAY 2 ★

TUESDAY 3 ★

WEDNESDAY 4

THURSDAY 5 ★ ● SUPER NOVA DAYS Focus on practical matters

FRIDAY 6 ★

SATURDAY 7 ★

SUNDAY 8 ★

MONDAY 9 ★

TUESDAY 10

WEDNESDAY 11

THURSDAY 12

FRIDAY 13

SATURDAY 14

SUNDAY 15

MONDAY 16 ★ You still may feel isolated or undeserving of love

---

TUESDAY 17 ★

WEDNESDAY 18 ★

THURSDAY 19 ★ ○

FRIDAY 20

SATURDAY 21

SUNDAY 22

MONDAY 23

TUESDAY 24

WEDNESDAY 25

THURSDAY 26 ★ There is beauty and opportunity everywhere you look

---

FRIDAY 27 ★

SATURDAY 28 ★

SUNDAY 29

MONDAY 30

TUESDAY 1 ★ Don't let your idealism turn into escapist behavior

WEDNESDAY 2 ★

THURSDAY 3 ★

FRIDAY 4 ★ ●

SATURDAY 5

SUNDAY 6

MONDAY 7

TUESDAY 8

WEDNESDAY 9

THURSDAY 10 ★ Things are neither as bad nor as good as they seem

FRIDAY 11 ★

SATURDAY 12 ★

SUNDAY 13

MONDAY 14

TUESDAY 15

WEDNESDAY 16 ★ Self-restraint and self-reflection are valuable now

THURSDAY 17 ★

FRIDAY 18 ★ ○

SATURDAY 19 ★

SUNDAY 20

MONDAY 21

TUESDAY 22

WEDNESDAY 23

THURSDAY 24

FRIDAY 25

SATURDAY 26

SUNDAY 27

MONDAY 28

TUESDAY 29 ★ **SUPER NOVA DAYS** There's very little margin for error

WEDNESDAY 30 ★

THURSDAY 31 ★

FRIDAY 1 ★ **SUPER NOVA DAYS** Initiate a difficult conversation

SATURDAY 2 ★

SUNDAY 3 ★ ●

MONDAY 4

TUESDAY 5

WEDNESDAY 6

THURSDAY 7

FRIDAY 8 ★ Turn on the charm

SATURDAY 9 ★

SUNDAY 10 ★

MONDAY 11 ★

TUESDAY 12 ★

WEDNESDAY 13

THURSDAY 14

FRIDAY 15

SATURDAY 16

SUNDAY 17 ★ ○ Keep trying until you get it right

MONDAY 18 ★

TUESDAY 19 ★

WEDNESDAY 20 ★

THURSDAY 21

FRIDAY 22

SATURDAY 23

SUNDAY 24

MONDAY 25

TUESDAY 26

WEDNESDAY 27 ★ Simplify your concept and explain everything carefully

THURSDAY 28 ★

FRIDAY 29 ★

SATURDAY 30 ★

SUNDAY 1 ★ Your intuition leads you in the right direction

MONDAY 2 ★ ●
TUESDAY 3 ★
WEDNESDAY 4
THURSDAY 5
FRIDAY 6
SATURDAY 7
SUNDAY 8
MONDAY 9
TUESDAY 10 ★ Your impatience creates problems

WEDNESDAY 11 ★
THURSDAY 12 ★
FRIDAY 13
SATURDAY 14
SUNDAY 15
MONDAY 16 ★ Focus on one task at a time now

TUESDAY 17 ★ ○
WEDNESDAY 18
THURSDAY 19
FRIDAY 20
SATURDAY 21
SUNDAY 22
MONDAY 23
TUESDAY 24 ★ Prepare to change your plans at a moment's notice

WEDNESDAY 25 ★
THURSDAY 26
FRIDAY 27
SATURDAY 28
SUNDAY 29 ★ **SUPER NOVA DAYS** Forgiveness is all that's truly important

MONDAY 30 ★
TUESDAY 31 ★

FAMOUS VIRGOS

River Phoenix	★	8/23/1970
Kobe Bryant	★	8/23/1978
Gene Kelly	★	8/23/1912
Dave Chappelle	★	8/24/1973
Regis Philbin	★	8/25/1933
Sean Connery	★	8/25/1930
Elvis Costello	★	8/25/1954
Claudia Schiffer	★	8/25/1970
Gene Simmons	★	8/25/1949
Mother Teresa	★	8/27/1910
Lyndon B. Johnson	★	8/27/1908
LeAnn Rimes	★	8/28/1982
Johann Wolfgang von Goethe	★	8/28/1749
Michael Jackson	★	8/29/1958
Ingrid Bergman	★	8/29/1915
Charlie Parker	★	8/29/1920
Clara Bow	★	8/29/1905
John McCain	★	8/29/1936
Preston Sturges	★	8/29/1898
Mary Wollstonecraft Shelley	★	8/30/1797
Andy Roddick	★	8/30/1982
Ted Williams	★	8/30/1918
Cameron Diaz	★	8/30/1972
Van Morrison	★	8/31/1945
Richard Gere	★	8/31/1949
Lily Tomlin	★	9/1/1939
Dr. Phil McGraw	★	9/1/1950
Rocky Marciano	★	9/1/1923
Keanu Reeves	★	9/2/1964
Lennox Lewis	★	9/2/1965
Salma Hayek	★	9/2/1966
Beyoncé Knowles	★	9/4/1981
Damon Wayans	★	9/4/1960
Mike Piazza	★	9/4/1968
Raquel Welch	★	9/5/1940
Freddie Mercury	★	9/5/1946
Rosie Perez	★	9/6/1964

FAMOUS VIRGOS

Buddy Holly	★	9/7/1936
Patsy Cline	★	9/8/1932
Peter Sellers	★	9/8/1925
Roger Waters	★	9/9/1943
Otis Redding	★	9/9/1941
Hugh Grant	★	9/9/1960
Arnold Palmer	★	9/10/1929
Randy Johnson	★	9/10/1963
D. H. Lawrence	★	9/11/1885
O. Henry	★	9/11/1862
Barry White	★	9/12/1944
Claudette Colbert	★	9/13/1903
Roald Dahl	★	9/13/1916
Agatha Christie	★	9/15/1890
Oliver Stone	★	9/15/1946
Prince Harry	★	9/15/1984
Lauren Bacall	★	9/16/1924
B. B. King	★	9/16/1925
Anne Bancroft	★	9/17/1931
Greta Garbo	★	9/18/1905
Frankie Avalon	★	9/18/1939
Lance Armstrong	★	9/18/1971
Trisha Yearwood	★	9/19/1964
Mama Cass Elliott	★	9/19/1941
Adam West	★	9/19/1928
Dr. Joyce Brothers	★	9/20/1928
Sophia Loren	★	9/20/1934
Upton Sinclair	★	9/20/1878
Bill Murray	★	9/21/1950
Faith Hill	★	9/21/1967
Stephen King	★	9/21/1947
H. G. Wells	★	9/21/1866
Joan Jett	★	9/22/1958
Andrea Bocelli	★	9/22/1958

VIRGO IN LOVE

VIRGO & ARIES (MARCH 21–APRIL 19)

Your personality is detail-oriented and analytical. You're a perfectionist who likes things to be done efficiently. You can be judgmental in ways that become self-defeating if not kept under control. Aries, however, lives a life that's somewhat looser. The Ram is a pioneer who pushes ahead with less organization and minimal emphasis on detail, which can irritate you. You'll find yourself judging irrepressible Aries as juvenile or simplistic, which isn't necessarily accurate. In spite of your great ability to focus on details, you can miss the bigger picture in life's everyday dramas. If the Moon in your chart is in a fire or air sign, you'll appreciate your Aries lover's zest for life. If your Moon is in an earth or water sign, you'll be more cautious to endorse your Ram's sense of immediacy. The bottom line is that Aries are movers and shakers—your life will not be dull if you partner with a Ram. Your sense of stability can help ground Aries, and you can make good business partners. If you can learn to accept your differences, you stand to learn much from happy Aries who can, in turn, light up your life.

VIRGO & TAURUS (APRIL 20–MAY 20)

You and Taurus can make a great pair, for you find a real companion in the Bull, who complements your analytical style with common sense. You are both earth signs and can encourage productivity in each other, especially in the realm of business and practical matters concerning home and family. Your heightened sense of perfectionism blends very well with the artistic and sensual tastes of your Taurus lover. If, however, your Venus is in Leo or Libra, you may have ongoing disagreements about what you each consider tasteful. In Taurus, you find someone who can create an environment that is clean, well-organized, and simplistically beautiful. Your partner will probably pay attention to money—balancing your frugal ways with their abundant desires. Your nature-loving Taurus will most likely also enjoy camping and outdoor hikes, and if they do love the outdoors, they may actually incorporate natural, earthy themes into home décor, including lots of plants and a useful herb or vegetable garden. This is a down-to-earth, no-nonsense match that can survive the toughest of times and thrive for many happy years.

VIRGO & GEMINI (MAY 21–JUNE 20)

Both you and Gemini have the planet Mercury as your ruling planet. Mercury is associated with all forms of communication, so words, ideas, and conversations are lively and emphasized in this relationship. Since you both love a well-crafted sentence, together you can revel in the beauty of speech and music. With all these similarities, you might think this is a match made in heaven, but your styles of communication are quite different. Your refined style is practical and highly critical, making you a talented editor. Meanwhile, your Gemini mate is comfortable when talking without a script, making him or her more social and very charming at parties. If your Mars is in a fire or air sign, you may feel at ease jumping into Gemini's clever conversations. But if your Mars is in a water or earth sign, you may have difficulty keeping up. Wherever your Mars is, you may find it hard to relax around your restless Gemini lover. You can burn off some of this energy by engaging in discussions about books, participating together in literary projects, or exploring new forms of communication. Romantic involvement with you two rationalists is both physical and mental. The right words can inspire much passion.

VIRGO & CANCER (JUNE 21–JULY 22)

You are tactful, well-mannered, and have a high-strung nervous system. You find much comfort within the protective sphere of a Cancer mate. You are apt to set the foundation for the home on the material plane by organizing and tidying up the environment. Your Cancer lover will warm and soften your cool aesthetic tastes with photos of friends, cozy blankets on chairs, and emotionally nurturing family memorabilia. The two of you must find a balance, however, because your Crab is sentimental, and in holding onto the past, can create clutter. You prefer neat and clean spaces—except when it's your own clutter, which isn't a mess, just an organized pile. Although you bring a rational point of view to your partner, he or she may not be as impressed with facts and figures as you are. This makes you crazy, for emotionally driven Cancers are more concerned with their gut intuition, and all the logic in the world isn't going to change their minds. If, however, the Moon in your chart is in a water sign, you may acknowledge the supremacy of intuition over logic. Nonetheless, communication flows well between you two; you'll be able to create many fond memories.

VIRGO & LEO (JULY 23–AUGUST 22)

You are very strong within your own self, even if you present a timid appearance. As such, you are not apt to need outside encouragement on a daily basis. And, because you have a sharp mind, you can be self-critical to a fault. You have, however, an uncanny endurance that gets you through most obstacles. Your sharp mind is connected to your sharp eye, and as such you can be overly critical of others, too. This doesn't fly with your Leo mate. The Lion cannot easily take criticism and may be in need of ongoing praise and attention, displaying strengths in other areas, such as devotion, love, and generosity. Your quiet humility may cause you to bump heads with the prideful Lion, who needs outward displays of affection to strengthen self-confidence and courage. If your chart has the Moon, Mercury, or Venus in Leo, you will be able to assimilate these leonine traits, using candor and humor to get around the irritations you may feel. Your Leo lover can appreciate your razor-sharp wit, but whatever you do, don't tease him or her. Handle Lions with respect and honor, even when they are displaying childlike tendencies, and you can find yourself in a winner of a relationship.

VIRGO & VIRGO (AUGUST 23–SEPT. 22)

When others are in the company of two Virgos, they may feel as though they are witnessing an elite club meeting in progress. You Virgos can find delight in each another for many reasons. You both see yourselves as slightly superior to the rest of the human race due to your innate organizational skills, acute detail in work, and your ability to execute ideas and put them to productive use. You are amazing, no doubt! No detail is too small to tackle or explain. The target problem areas of the relationship develop when your fastidious minds compete as to which one of the two will rule the roost. You both have set and exacting ideas, but they may differ widely, especially if Mercury is in different signs in your individual charts. If, however, they are in the same sign, your ideas may be more complementary, balanced, and cooperative. This mutual and shared intellectual perspective will allow for peace and happiness. There is good wit and humor shared between you two, but it is usually on the dry side. This relationship may function well and have an efficient practicality, but it's probably not going to be very warm and fuzzy.

VIRGO & LIBRA (SEPT. 23–OCT. 22)

You are as reflective, analytical, and refined as your Libra lover and can get along famously, as long as Libra isn't too wishy-washy when it comes to making decisions. You'll probably get annoyed with the indecision of your partner, who would rather avoid picking one option over another. Libra will feel pressured by you, even if that's not your intention. Libra will feel judged under your critically discerning eye. But it's not just about making decisions. You may also be critical of his or her laziness. And, unless you have Mercury or Venus in Libra in your chart, you'll probably think your Libra mate isn't very practical . . . and you'll be right! Libras are more interested in aesthetics than utility. Your Libra will want the walls painted white because it looks better, but you'll want them a light ivory because dirt won't show up as quickly. Actually, you are both keen on beauty and balance, and can build a lovely environment that others find refreshing, clean, and stimulating. Together, you can be prosperous and indulge in the finer things in life. With some individual adjustments, this can be a compatible relationship with good potential.

VIRGO & SCORPIO (OCT. 23–NOV. 21)

You appreciate tact, as well as a well-groomed environment. You dislike anything crude or unpolished, preferring to relate with people who will not offend or embarrass your sense of decency. Your Scorpio partner, although quiet and deeply honest, may at times step over the line of acceptability for your taste. Overtly blunt, and not afraid to venture deep into the mysterious dark edges of life, your passionate Scorpio mate is driven to plunge into experiences with unedited intensity. Let's face it: you are attracted to Scorpio's frank and honest personality, but you wish your mate could be emotionally more mellow. You will have to get past the manner in which your lover presents his or her views, or your refined nature may feel overwhelmed. Sometimes Scorpio's volcanic power actually scares you, unless you have the Moon in a water sign, like Scorpio. If you do, you will feel more at home with the depths of your partner's emotional realms. The two of you will be honest with each other, and will most likely enjoy diving into the caverns of the psyche as a means of churning up the details of the unconscious.

VIRGO & SAGITTARIUS (NOV. 22–DEC. 21)

Your character tends to be service-oriented with a keen awareness of your duties and responsibilities. You are exacting in the way you deal with the mundane tasks of everyday life and are a great asset at work and at home. The Sagittarius nature is dramatically different than yours, for they tend to be more broad-minded with sweeping goals and ambitions. Your Sagittarius partner is humorous, enthusiastic, and good-natured. He or she tries to make the best out of every situation. Under pressure, you focus on the little things, while the Archer aims the arrow of consciousness into the grand outer world. Your tendency may be to pull in to protect yourself in response to your mate's plans to travel or conquer the world. But if you can get past basic differences, the two of you can work effectively as a team, organizing the details of life with an open-minded awareness. Your chances for long-term compatibility are improved if the Moon in your chart is in a fire or air sign. If you can harmonize your wonderful potentials, the two of you should be able to enjoy the pursuit of shared social and intellectual activities with great interest and success.

VIRGO & CAPRICORN (DEC. 22–JAN. 19)

You're normally hesitant in your actions until you know that everything is proper. Your Capricorn lover is also conservative in action and carefully plans goals and then sets out to achieve them. You are both cautious about matters of the heart. As you tend toward critical thinking, you bring a sharp flavor of communication into relationships. To others, you can appear cool and distant. This works well with your Goat, for Capricorn is also well-guarded at the beginning of a relationship. Capricorns do not wear their heart on their sleeve and can hold back feelings until it appears very safe. Your partner is probably more serious than you are. If Venus in your chart is in Leo, you might find this seriousness too much. If your Venus is in Libra, you may not relate to Capricorn's belief that practicality is more important than beauty. In any event, your organizational abilities should blend nicely with Capricorn's ordered, but sometimes controlling, way of life. For the most part, you'll enjoy sharing the same space and can easily adjust to each other's habits. Romantic fires may take a while to get roaring, yet both of you can be very affectionate and sexy once you've moved past your issues of trust and have learned how to share.

VIRGO & AQUARIUS (JAN. 20–FEB. 18)

You have a very strong work ethics and are a service-oriented type of person. You have a deep desire to help others and are happiest when you're working efficiently at your tasks. Aquarius cares deeply about the greater community and is the humanitarian of the zodiac. Together, you can make waves and have an impact working with organizations, doing most any kind of group activity that involves high standards and shared values. That being said, there are some formidable differences. You are a practical, detail-oriented worker, whereas your Aquarius lover likes abstract intellectual principles. If you can stay open, Virgo, you stand to gain from the "big picture" that your Aquarius offers. If you aren't too critical, you can benefit from the many new friends that your partner brings into your life. If, however, you have Mars in a fire or air sign, then you may actually be as outgoing as your eclectic Aquarius mate. Ultimately, your Aquarius lover needs to relate with intelligent people, and you qualify on this account— you're not only a suitable mate, but your clear thinking can be quite inspiring to your partner. If nothing else, you two make compatible friends—of course, this compatibility can go much further.

VIRGO & PISCES (FEB. 19–MARCH 20)

Sometimes opposites do attract, and there's no doubt about it: Pisces is your opposite. You are exacting and disciplined where Pisces can be scattered and spacey. You are rational and logical while Pisces is imaginative and emotional. You respond to life's circumstances by narrowing your focus, analyzing the details as you figure out your next move. Your Pisces lover discards obvious facts while searching inward, relying on intuition instead of data. If the Moon in your chart is in a water sign, then you'll be more open to the imaginal realms of your Pisces. If the Moon in your chart is in an earth sign, you may think that Pisces is just too flaky for you. You may get annoyed at what you consider escapist tendencies in your lover, although he or she may not see it that way. If, however, you can accept your differences, you can actually be of great help to each other, as you each bring balance into the areas of life that are weak for the other. In fact, you can serve as mirrors to each other's souls. This relationship softens you and teaches you how to become more compassionate. You can teach your Fish how to productively organize his or her life. Together, you can be very sweet and loving.

ABOUT THE AUTHORS

RICK LEVINE When I first encountered astrology as a psychology undergraduate in the late 1960s, I became fascinated with the varieties of human experience. Even now, I love the one-on-one work of seeing clients and looking at their lives through the cosmic lens. But I also love history and utilize astrology to better understand the longer-term cycles of cultural change. My recent DVD, *Quantum Astrology*, explores some of these transpersonal interests. As a scientist, I'm always looking for patterns in order to improve my ability to predict the outcome of any experiment; as an artist, I'm entranced by the mystery of what we do not and cannot know. As an astrologer, I am privileged to live in an enchanted world that links the rational and magical, physical and spiritual—and yes—even science and art.

JEFF JAWER I'm a Taurus with a Scorpio Moon and Aries rising who lives in the Pacific Northwest with Danick, my double-Pisces musician wife, our two Leo daughters, a black Gemini cat, and a white Pisces dog. I have been a professional astrologer since 1973 when I was a student at the University of Massachusetts (Amherst). I encountered astrology as my first marriage was ending and I was searching for answers. Astrology provided them. More than thirty-five years later, it remains the creative passion of my life as I continue to counsel, write, study, and share ideas with clients and colleagues around the world.

ACKNOWLEDGMENTS

Thanks to Paul O'Brien, our agent, our friend, and the creative genius behind Tarot.com; Gail Goldberg, the editor who always makes us sound better; Marcus Leaver and Michael Fragnito at Sterling Publishing, for their tireless support for the project; Barbara Berger, our supervising editor, who has shepherded this book with Taurean persistence and Aquarian invention; Laura Jorstad, for her refinement of the text; and Sterling project editor Mary Hern, assistant editor Sasha Tropp, and designer Abrah Griggs for their invaluable help. We thank Bob Wietrak and Jules Herbert at Barnes & Noble, and all of the helping hands at Sterling. Thanks for the art and ideas from Jessica Abel and the rest of the Tarot.com team. Thanks as well to 3+Co. for the original design and to Tara Gimmer for the author photo.